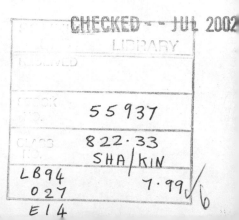

# THE CRITICS DEBATE

### General Editor: Michael Scott

**The Critics Debate**

General Editor: Michael Scott

Published titles:

**Sons and Lovers** Geoffrey Harvey

**Bleak House** Jeremy Hawthorn

**The Canterbury Tales** Alcuin Blamires

**Tess of the d'Urbervilles** Terence Wright

**Hamlet** Michael Hattaway

**The Waste Land and Ash Wednesday**
    Arnold P. Hinchliffe

**Paradise Lost** Margarita Stocker

**King Lear** Ann Thompson

**Othello** Peter Davison

**The Winter's Tale** Bill Overton

**Gulliver's Travels** Brian Tippett

**Blake: Songs of Innocence and Experience**
    David Lindsay

**Measure for Measure** T. F. Wharton

**The Tempest** David Daniell

Further titles are in preparation.

# CORIOLANUS

## Bruce King

**MACMILLAN**

To Leela and Dom

First published 1989

Published by
MACMILLAN EDUCATION LTD
Houndmills, Basingstoke, Hampshire RG21 2XS
and London
Companies and representatives
throughout the world

Typeset by Wessex Typesetters
(Division of The Eastern Press Ltd)
Frome, Somerset

Printed in Hong Kong


British Library Cataloguing in Publication Data
King, Bruce, 1933–
Coriolanus.—(The Critics debate).
1. Drama in English. Shakespeare, William,
1564–1616. Coriolanus. Critical studies
I. Title  II. Series
822.3'3
ISBN 0–333–46730–2
ISBN 0–333–46731–0 Pbk

# Contents

*General Editor's Preface*                                                    7
*A Note on Text and References*                                               9
*Introduction*                                                              10

**Part One: Survey**

Contextual approaches                                                        13
Textual and formal approaches: character and imagery                         17
Religious, sociological and anthropological approaches                       31
Interdisciplinary approaches                                                 43
Theatre approaches: performance                                              50

**Part Two: Appraisal: Methodological Problems**

Post-modernist theory or Jacobean theatre of mirrors?                        60
Staging and some conventions                                                 61
The crowd                                                                    63
Seven scenes of warfare: Act i.iv–x                                          64
Distancing                                                                   66
An historical style: the house of mirrors                                    66
The isolated hero's tragedy                                                  67
The hero, society and honour                                                 68
Shakespeare's recurrent themes and techniques                               72
Language and acting as deception                                            75
Revelations of character                                                     76
Coriolanus and his mother                                                    76
Persuasion and dependency                                                    80
Crying                                                                       82
Sex, love and bonding                                                        83

The virgin warrior: fear of contamination                84
The price of love: unclean mouths                        85
Pretending love: inconstancy                             87
The sexuality of battle                                  88
The sexuality of domination                              89
Power                                                    90
Act v.vi                                                 93
Coriolanus' death                                        95
Comedy?                                                  97
The politics of neo-classicism                           98
Social context                                          100
Coriolanus and monarchy                                 103
Conclusion                                              104

*References*                                            108
*Selected Bibliography*                                 111
*Index*                                                 112

# General Editor's Preface

OVER THE last few years the practice of literary criticism has become hotly debated. Methods developed earlier in the century and before have been attacked and the word 'crisis' has been drawn upon to describe the present condition of English Studies. That such a debate is taking place is a sign of the subject discipline's health. Some would hold that the situation necessitates a radical alternative approach which naturally implies a 'crisis situation'. Others would respond that to employ such terms is to precipitate or construct a false position. The debate continues but it is not the first. 'New Criticism' acquired its title because it attempted something fresh, calling into question certain practices of the past. Yet the practices it attacked were not entirely lost or negated by the new critics. One factor becomes clear: English Studies is a pluralistic discipline.

What are students coming to advanced work in English for the first time to make of all this debate and controversy? They are in danger of being overwhelmed by the cross-currents of critical approaches as they take up their study of literature. The purpose of this series is to help delineate various critical approaches to specific literary texts. Its authors are from a variety of critical schools and have approached their task in a flexible manner. Their aim is to help the reader come to terms with the variety of criticism and to introduce him or her to further reading on the subject and to a fuller evaluation of a particular text by illustrating the way it has been approached in a number of contexts. In the first part of the book a critical survey is given of some of the major ways the text has been appraised. This is done sometimes in a thematic manner, sometimes according to various 'schools' or 'approaches'. In the second part the authors provide their own appraisals of the text from their stated critical standpoint, allowing the reader the knowledge of their own particular approaches from which their views may in turn be evaluated. The series therein hopes to introduce and to elucidate criticism of authors and texts being studied and to encourage participation as the critics debate.

*Michael Scott*

# A Note on Text and References

ALL REFERENCES to *Coriolanus* are to the Macmillan Shakespeare edition, edited by Tony Parr (London and Basingstoke, 1985). References to secondary material appear with the date of publication on the introduction of each such work. Details may then be found in the References section where secondary works are listed in the order of first citation in the text.

# Introduction

EARLY IN THIS century A. C. Bradley claimed that
*Coriolanus* was seldom acted and that except for educational
purposes it was seldom read. Taste has changed and *Coriolanus*
is now often seen on stage and has received considerable
critical attention; but it remains a problem to many people
because of its lack of an obviously sympathetic character or
cause with which the reader or spectator might identify.
Whether we speak of distancing, epic theatre or use the
Brechtian notion of alienation, *Coriolanus* seems very modern
in its unwillingness either to take sides or offer much sympathy
for its characters. We are given an excess of information
without guidance as to how we are to view what we learn. Its
central conflict between individual aspirations and communal
cohesion has been at the centre of our culture since the
Romantics, and is often interpreted in contemporary terms as
some version of the political right against the left, but could
as easily be seen as individual freedom versus social control.
*Coriolanus* has another claim to be considered modern or even
post-modern in its self-reflectivity and self-consciousness of
the art of making fictions. The concern in the play with acting,
role-playing, persuasion, directing scenes, rhetoric and trials,
seems to call attention to the falsity of theatre, and questions
the premeditated use of language. The characteristics that
make *Coriolanus* contemporary for us confuse those who prefer
texts more straightforward in their attitudes or which can be
translated into obvious sympathies. Many people are so
surprised by the distancing and by disagreeable characteristics
of Coriolanus that they dislike the play; but eventually they
become convinced that it is one of Shakespeare's greatest
works.
   Criticism should address problems of the kind of play

*Coriolanus* is, how we see or read it, what is the effect of the distancing on our response, how does this play fit into Shakespeare's work, what kind of social and political pressures have gone into it, and what it is like in the theatre. Self-awareness of the basis of criticism is of particular relevance now that Critical Theory is in fashion and has challenged pragmatic, empirical, practical criticism. Practical criticism and the analysis of patterns of imagery, or the New Critic emphasis on tensions, irony and ambiguity reflected the modern literature of the time; they were useful methods for reading T. S. Eliot, James Joyce and Dylan Thomas as well as Shakespeare. Recent theoretical approaches came into fashion along with the post-modernism of Alain Robbe-Grillet, Jorges L. Borges and the view that literature is concerned with the processes and nature of literature, rather than the imitation of reality. As literature and culture change so does criticism; our vocabulary, understanding of technique, our way of conceptualising, will have different built-in assumptions than in the past. Indeed, there is a school of reception criticism which argues that the interpretation of literature is the history of interpretation – the meaning of a text is how it is viewed at various times.

We need not become lost in problems of whether such a history is not itself a fiction; there are surprising consistencies in the history of the interpretation of *Coriolanus*. The same questions recur. Does the play have a moral concerning obedience to government? Is the hero so disagreeable and excessive in his warrior values as to be the villain of the piece, or is he admirable for his attempt to live up to an heroic ideal? What does Shakespeare think of the citizens and the tribunes? Why does Coriolanus turn from a patriot defending Rome into someone intent on destroying it? And why does he relent? We have an idea how the last two questions can be answered. In terms of plot, Coriolanus seeks revenge and is then persuaded by his mother that to destroy Rome would both destroy his reputation and lead to the destruction of his own family. But we want better, more satisfying answers, perhaps from psychology or political theory. The imagery and subtexts push us away from mere narrative towards other kinds of readings; the distancing requires a conceptualisation of our response. What kinds of questions are we asking and why?

In the following pages I am not primarily interested in listing the sympathies and opinions of critics towards the characters in *Coriolanus*. Such readings are predictable: each critic claims that the previous one wrongly assumed that Shakespeare was a liberal, socialist, fascist, when in fact he held similar views to that of the critic you are reading. It seems to me more useful to understand how kinds of critical discussion are generated, what light they throw on *Coriolanus*, their limitations, and what other approaches or analyses might be useful.

# Part One: Survey

CRITICISM is shaped by conventions or the prejudices of those who criticise. Because of their assumptions some critics will only see class warfare in *Coriolanus*: still others will construct a novel involving the emotions of the characters as they interact on each other. The main critical approaches to literature are contextual, formal or textual, sociological, religious, and interdisciplinary (Marxist, psychological, etc.). While political, social and religious studies can be contextual, they are approaches on their own if distinguished from simple historicism. Each extended work of art depicts or reflects some society, shows or assumes some religion or cosmology. Theatre and production studies might be regarded as textual or formal approaches, but I will treat them separately as they are central to my discussion of *Coriolanus*.

## Contextual approaches

### *Biographical and topical*

Contextual criticism is usually some version of historicism and the main question is the kind of context constructed in which to see the work or author. Biographical criticism, which is a version of historicising a context, is of little use for discussing Shakespeare. We know a number of facts about Shakespeare's life but not enough about him as a person to guess what emotions might have gone into his play and poems. For *Coriolanus* the only connection is that Shakespeare's mother died the year we think the play was written. It is possible that this found its way into Coriolanus' affection for his mother; but as can be seen by *Hamlet* and *King Lear* Shakespeare was for some time writing plays about the destructive effects of excessive emotional attachments between children and parents.

Possible parallels between the rebellious heroism of Coriolanus and the lives of such Elizabethans and Jacobeans as the Irish Earl Tyrone, Essex and Sir Walter Raleigh are discussed by Holt (1976). They are too vague to be more than examples of Renaissance individualism. Holt also summarises the arguments of Pettet (1950) and others who argue the relationship between the play and the Jacobean enclosure riots. This obviously is a source for the emphasis Shakespeare gives to drought and shortage of grains in *Coriolanus*. More important it seems the start of Shakespeare's imagery concerning food, nourishment, care, and love. Information about enclosure riots can be found most conveniently in Bullough (1964). Source studies may at first appear convincing, but they are of limited use. The mutiny over grain is significant in Shakespeare's play as an example of inequalities of Roman society; but once the people have been given representatives they forget the grain shortage.

Critics have not found much of interest in Shakespeare's use of his classical sources, although it is sometimes suggested that the classicism and artistic restraint of *Coriolanus* owes much to the closeness with which the dramatist followed Plutarch. An interest in Rome was, however, part of an antiquarianism or historicism which was developing at the turn of the century. Perhaps the leading scholar who did most to show a Roman presence still visible in England was William Camden (Ben Jonson's teacher) from whose *Remaines of a Greater Worke concerning Britaine* (1605), Bullough says, 'Shakespeare took a point or two . . . for Menenius' fable of the belly and its members'. That Shakespeare wrote three Roman plays at this time (the others being *Julius Caesar, Antony and Cleopatra*) and Ben Jonson wrote two Roman plays (*Catiline* and *Sejanus*) seems significant to Spencer (1957) and Honig (1951) who examine the Jonsonian context while Huffman sees Jonson and Shakespeare both influenced by James I's use of Roman analogies in his political theories.

*Political*

Although the political context has been discussed at length, such studies seem barely to touch the play. Having with detail tried to put *Coriolanus* in a political context through the study of the writings of James I, Huffman (1971) claims: 'Shakespeare the dramatist of the King's Men who had already deliberately written plays that spoke to James's interests, had in the court climate itself not only the subject of a political drama but also a clear indication of the treatment he ought to give.' Huffman then offers a reading of *Coriolanus* to prove that a play put on at the Globe and Blackfriars theatres by the King's Men necessarily opposes political innovation and is conservative in tendency. Writing about early Rome, Shakespeare chose one consonant with King James' royalist view of it as a rivalry between absolute monarchy and democracy, between rule and misrule, between order and chaos. Huffman treats each detail as having such a significance. 'The presentation of the now-evil tribunes who continue to demonstrate their evil though the rest of the play corresponds to King James's view of his opponents in the House of Commons.' A footnote remarks that Plutarch contains nothing of Coriolanus' extreme dislike of seeking the people's votes; 'there may be in this characteristic a reflection of James's well-known dislike of crowds of commoners'. It is unconvincing to argue from such weak evidence that *Coriolanus* was written to James' taste. Huffman goes further. Coriolanus' extreme attitudes are wrong because the Stuart king would not approve. 'Coriolanus is the only patrician who cannot respond to the ideal of Temperance, which is the more important not only because of its place in the Graeco-Roman and Christian traditions, but also because King James so strongly urged it.' Huffman claims to understand how Shakespeare's audience might have understood Coriolanus' banishment and revenge. 'In Shakespeare, then, approval is accorded foreign invasion only if it has positive, even religious, associations and does not thereafter harm the country.' Elaborate research here produces commonplaces, triviality, or fog. Huffman neither suggests enough parallels between the play and the politics of the time to show a topicality, nor does he try to examine how

the social and political tensions of the period might have been
transformed into the Coriolanus story through the mediation
of Roman history. Instead we have the crude assumption that
the play was written to James' taste and that when in doubt
we must ask what James would have thought. James becomes
a master myth, which explains everything.

### History of ideas

*Coriolanus* should yield easily to historical contextual
approaches. Its themes of revenge and mercy, use of the
grotesque, its satiric main character, the shift in perspectives,
the lack of compassion and sympathy, the way everyone seems
wrong and we end baffled, has many similarities to Jacobean
drama by Marston, Middleton, Tourneur, while the wry use
of historical materials is Jonsonian. Yet there has been little
critical discussion of the play in the context of specifically
Jacobean theatre conventions, although we will later find
Dollimore offers a Marxist perspective on the drama of the
period. Siegel (1968) examines *Coriolanus* within 'The Neo-
Chivalric Cult of Honor'. He is concerned with a supposed
conflict between two major ethical systems, Christianity and
a revived Graeco-Roman humanism. The Christian humanist
comes into conflict with an ideal of the medieval knight as
expounded by the Tudor aristocracy; an older feudal idea is
in conflict with capitalism. According to Siegel, Coriolanus
suffers from an obsession with honour, not of pride. At the
end of the play, not abiding by the dictates of the neo-chivalric
cult of honour which call for revenge even against one's
country and parents he is transformed into a god of forgiveness:
'like Christ, he dies as a result of treachery on the part of one
of his associates'. As Siegel's methods seem to require him to
offer a unified interpretation – pride *or* honour – this gets a
bit confused, although he has interestingly teased out the
mercy-Christ analogy from the play.

   That there was a sharpened notion of honour in the sixteenth
and seventeenth centuries is clear from the plays and poems
of the time. That it necessarily resulted from two major ethical
systems coming together is questionable; ethical systems

themselves are influenced by social or political changes. The commonplace that the change is between feudal and capitalist systems is about as useful as fate, destiny or the rise of the middle class. It would be better to look for specific social changes, such as the rise of a European high court culture with the end of Feudalism and the centralisation of the state. Another possible context is instability of the English nobility in the Jacobean period. The Tudors did what they could to lessen the strength and number of lords. James I rapidly increased the number of lords and sold titles. Jacobean England was an unsettled society with anxieties about identity, honour, title, and manliness.

## Textual and formal approaches: character and imagery

### Fictionalising Coriolanus

Contextual studies have been of little use to understanding *Coriolanus*. Better criticism has been concerned with matters directly arising from the reading of the text of the play (character, images, themes, irony, form, structure). Modern Shakespeare criticism begins in the study of character. The study of character itself developed out of the nineteenth-century focus on the individual, unity of selfhood, a belief in the sense of self which is the heart of nineteenth-century fiction. Jane Austen expects consistency of the self as a moral quality: D. H. Lawrence, Proust and twentieth-century novelists generally see the self as unstable, influenced by emotions, context, the irrational, the repressed. Much twentieth-century Shakespeare criticism works through alternative ways of regarding the self and the world. What is Coriolanus? A patrician warrior true to himself and the code he has been taught? Why is he rejected by the community he claims to represent? Why, having refused to humiliate himself before the Roman citizenry to be elected to the highest office, does he at the end of the play seek to win over the enemy Volscians by the very rhetorical tricks he disdained before?

The classic and most important treatment of *Coriolanus* as character study is A. C. Bradley's lecture (1912). It is significant that Bradley feels uncomfortable with the play and thus looks forward to the need for other approaches to examine the problems he raises. He begins by noting that the play is not popular. The main character's faults are repellent; there is no compensating imaginative effect, such as the supernatural. Shakespeare has totally secularised the world. He has also avoided that other source of pleasure, the 'exhibition of inward conflict', those outbursts of passion when a character, such as Richard II or Hamlet, becomes a great poet. Coriolanus is passionate but not imaginative; he transfigures nothing with the magic of poetry. His eloquence is vituperation and scorn. His deepest feelings are almost dumb; they govern his life but he does not speak about them. When he gives in to his mother and his own fate is decided, he hardly says anything; his inner emotions are hidden from us.

Bradley claims that while political conflict is never the centre of interest in Shakespeare's play, here is a play in which a prominent element is conflict between democracy and aristocracy. He tries to excuse Shakespeare of undemocratic views in portrayal of the citizens. There is no reason to ascribe to Shakespeare any particular politics (i.e. he is not anti-democratic) since the representation of the people is part of 'a dramatic design'. As Bradley develops the notion, it sounds too much like a 'heads I win, tails you lose' argument; there must be sympathy and faults on both sides in drama. If the hero is to be given a reason why he feels he must destroy Rome then there need be strong provocations.

Bradley's character studies of the citizens, Coriolanus, Aufidius and others reveal a wish to avoid controversy or conflict with public opinion. The citizens 'are fundamentally good-natured, like the Englishmen they are'. (But they are Romans!) Bradley notices that Coriolanus' politics are not shared by other patricians. The patricians will reluctantly accept the tribunes; Coriolanus will not. Coriolanus' view of the state is such that it would be 'dangerous' to appoint him consul as he does not acknowledge the political rights of the people. Bradley, however, is soon off in the realm of comforting platitudes. His Coriolanus seems a nineteenth-century English gentleman: Coriolanus is not a tyrant; he is really an aristocrat. Coriolanus treats his fellow patricians as equals because they share his breeding and values. By contrast the plebeians do not share his values 'and they do not even clean their teeth'.

### Fictionalising versus epic distance

Bradley constructs an old-fashioned novel, filled with easy psychology and moral judgements. Coriolanus is unjust and narrow, but magnificently true to his ideals. He reminds us of a huge boy with a fine sense of honour who is too simple and noble to explain himself. He is ignorant of himself, and proud but unaware of his pride. When Coriolanus is exiled, he 'is still excited and exalted by conflict'. But 'Days go by, and no one, not even his Mother hears a word'. 'As time passes, and no suggestion of recall reaches Coriolanus, and he learns what it is to be a solitary homeless exile, his heart hardens, his pride swells to a mountainous bulk, and the wound in it becomes a fire. The fellow-patricians from whom he parted lovingly now appear to him ingrates and dastards, scarcely better than the loathsome mob.'

This is pure speculation as to time and motives. It is a fiction created by the critic. Worse, it completely ignores what makes *Coriolanus* so effective; as there is a gap where Coriolanus' character seems to change, we never do understand him, just as we never exactly understand why he later gives in to his mother and spares Rome. Where Shakespeare offers ambiguity and unexplained depth of human character, Bradley wants to explain.

What happens to Coriolanus off stage we do not know. That is inherent in the epic theatre Shakespeare inherited from the medieval mystery play; but it is also a technique he developed further in his later plays. *Hamlet* has a similar gap in the centre. We do not know what motivates the Duke in *Measure for Measure*. Iago gives so many motives for his behaviour that we believe in none. Why cannot Cordelia speak? Some of Shakespeare's great tragedies foreground psychology – *Othello*, for example – others purposefully obscure motivation. Whatever the reason, several of the tragedies, especially the Roman plays, take epic distancing further, making it almost a new technique. *Coriolanus* takes this very far. Bradley by trying to explain character in terms of commonsense psychology reduces Coriolanus to a hurt schoolboy. But he embodies social tensions, repressed primitive emotions, communal rituals and more. Bradley reduces complexity into one easy judgement. 'Though this play is by no means a drama of destiny we might almost say that Volumnia is responsible for the hero's life and death.' 'Her sense of personal honour . . . was less keen than his; but she was much more patriotic.' In Bradley's lectures on Shakespeare we see an acute mind, an accurate reader, turning complexity into easily manageable cliches, reducing the ambiguity of art into commonplaces. But because he was intelligent, observant and aware that the play was not giving him what he expected, Bradley raised many of the problems which later criticism would discuss. Like Samuel Johnson he often seems to be at his most useful when we disagree with his judgements.

Many later critics follow in Bradley's footsteps, novelising Shakespeare's play, and less consciously seeking simple explanations, assuming a unity of character, confusing the text with what the reader wants and demanding sympathy with the hero. When that does not exist in a simple way, the critic creates either an interpretation which offers a sympathetic Coriolanus or a likeable mob. There is a failure here in accepting the epic mode, in accepting the nature of Shakespeare's experiments with distancing in his tragedies, an unwillingness to accept that Shakespeare's view might be highly pessimistic, cynical, cruel or that he might even have no views which he tried to offer. Bradley assumes a direct relationship between what is seen and Shakespeare. There is no mediation, no mirror or indirect reflection. If the mobs in the play are unfair, Shakespeare must dislike democracy and as, of course, we cannot accept that this is so, it is necessary to find reasons which explain why he shows mobs as unfair.

One reason why Bradleyism continues beyond our desire for characters we can sympathise with is that readers of literature create fictions, we create narratives to explain what is unexplained. We find it difficult to live with chaos, with the fragmentation of life, so we create patterns, stories, myths, allegories, narratives which give meaning to what otherwise lacks meaning or is unmanageable. Shakespeare, in these later plays, exploits our instinct to make fictions by leaving spaces, by offering contradictory explanations, using juxtapositions. He has learned to show not explain; he does not include the connections.

*Character, narrative and practical criticism*

Bradleyism, the creation of a simple character to fill in what Shakespeare left unsaid or what he showed to be complex and multilayered, and perhaps unexplainable, is the staple of most practical criticism interpretations. Practical criticism does not necessarily lead in that direction but once critics feel the need to explain each line of a poem or play they are likely to seek consistency, unity, and create versions of a story about a patrician and his relationship to his mother and the people; why he seeks and does not carry out his revenge. The better critics, like Vickers (1976), understand that the story is sophisticated by ironic contradictions and parallels, that we see characters through different eyes and therefore the motivation of the speaker must be taken into account. But essentially, practical critics offer a better version of the same kind of fiction, the complexity of life reduced to a manageable narrative with simple psychology and unity of character (although a unity which now includes paradoxes). An effective way for such a critic to operate is to reverse whatever the consensus is at the moment.

Bayley (1981) shows how the game is played. 'Coriolanus could be said to be far more successful in the role of husband and lover than he is in that of soldier and statesman.' 'Like all men who back into the limelight Coriolanus is genuinely embarrassed and miserable when surrounded by an admiring crowd.' Menenius 'has a genuine love for Coriolanus; it is one of the most attractive things about him.' 'Coriolanus is lovable, except to his own mother, whose egotism is proof against any capacity to be really aware of him as a person.' 'Shakespeare here is portraying a kind of class inflexibility common in various ways in all ages and societies. It is even necessary, even beneficial: the self-respect of both parties may depend on it.'

Bayley's remarks are Bradleyian fictionalising, the making up or explaining of character, plus simple judgements and class prejudices disguised as appeals to commonsense. He assumes unity of character, is not much interested in technique, the art of the play or the context which produced it. The play is a comedy, a 'reassertion of human weakness and the tolerations it needs'. 'Coriolanus is human, after all.' Bayley assumes that Coriolanus has backed into the limelight, that someone of that sort is 'genuinely' embarrassed when admired, that Coriolanus is lovable, that Coriolanus does not brag of his ancestry and achievement, and that 'class inflexibility' is good. This sounds more like the expected behaviour of a Tory leader or someone who might be elected master of an Oxford college; it better describes a member of the British upper middle class than the insulting, abrasive, often angry victorious warrior seen in parts of the play. Shakespeare's complex, fragmented unknowable Coriolanus has been turned into a caricature Englishman, even with a recognisable upper-middle-class English mother. The defence of 'class inflexibility' is worthy of Menenius. Bayley's analysis of Coriolanus' character seems a typical blow in the push and shove of English class attitudes.

### Imported assumptions and prejudices

*Coriolanus* brings out class prejudices. John Palmer's (1945) voice of consensus belongs to the early years of the Labour government after the war. 'Second Citizen pleads for Marcius with a magnaminity which is very creditable in a hungry man.' The citizens accept Menenius 'a noble Roman who has a decent regard for their interests'. 'There is no bad blood between them, and, on the popular side, a readiness to consider the other fellow's point of view.' Palmer's interpretation of Shakespeare's play assumes that the world he knows is the world of the past and that Shakespeare's attitudes or beliefs are directly available through a character. 'Menenius is Shakespeare's portrait of an average member of the privileged class in any community, the speaking likeness of an English squire removed to a Roman setting.' Palmer obviously has not known members of privileged classes outside England and other western democracies. But in any case the original Menenius in Plutarch is liked by the labourers because his origins were in that class rather than the patricians. Palmer however says Menenius can 'talk to the people as one man to another because he is entirely assured of his position'; by contrast Coriolanus is 'an aristocrat . . . who has a blind contempt for the common man and is impatient of any claim to consideration or fair dealing put forward by persons not of his own class.' If Coriolanus is not someone whom you would wish to have in your club, the tribunes are Shakespeare's 'counterfeit' presentation of two labour leaders 'they have neither the wish, training nor ability to discuss the quality or intention of their activities. In working for their party they do not claim to be working disinterestedly for the nation. In resorting to the lawful and customary tricks of the political trade they neglect the noble postures and impressive mimicries adopted by persons with a longer experience of public life and of the deportment which public life requires.' In Palmer's battle of polite snobberies you show your superiority by understanding the reasons for the other side's faults. Poor Coriolanus is not going to be much respected by such alliance of patrician noblesse oblige with Labour government.

It would be dangerous if at the end of the day *Coriolanus* turns out really to be about politics, so instead it is neutered. Palmer concludes 'that Shakespeare, who gave to the stage a gallery of political characters unequalled in any literature for their historical veracity, had no great interest in public affairs. He was interested in persons and many of them just happen to have been public persons.' And that whimper is the final reason to suspect character analysis, at least as practised in English criticism, as unable to see cultural products in any depth or to look behind them to what produced them. Palmer and Bayley tell more about expected behaviour in England among the middle and upper classes than about *Coriolanus*. 'Shakespeare had no particular admiration for success in public life.' How does Palmer know? Palmer claims 'Shakespeare had no political bias.' How does he know? This is not criticism. From Bradley's struggle with a play that is contrary to what he wants I learn much about the play. From Palmer and Bayley I learn about the way British social attitudes shape what people want to see when reading a play.

## Imagery – textual

The most important literary critic in Shakespeare studies after Bradley was G. Wilson Knight, who influenced both criticism and productions for two decades from the mid-1930s on, both through his own writings and through his influence on L. C. Knights and other critics associated with *Scrutiny* including F. R. Leavis. Knight believed a Shakespearean play was an expanded poetic metaphor. As he was not interested in the historical context, narrative, characterisation, and treated literature as patterns, especially of images and themes, Knight has been called a structuralist ahead of his time. There is certainly that side to Knight's criticism. But there were other interesting aspects that are now neglected. Knight acted, wrote of acting and production, and he had notions about rhythmic body movement and the reduction of the stage to a plain but highly symbolic set. There is also the spiritualistic side of Knight which he hid but which emerged in his criticism as large philosophical themes and in rejected romantic Christ-like heroes who struggled with evil. His artist-hero-devil had to do evil to bring about a greater good. So each work of literature consists of patterns of images and themes and a deeply structured allegory.

In the 1951 edition of *The Imperial Theme* (1931) Knight says he favoured a new precision in the handling of imagery and symbol, an 'insistence on the unity of the Shakespeare play', and that he is concerned with poetic interpretation as distinguished from criticism. Knight saw himself as studying Shakespeare's work as an organic whole, as poetry in its totality, in contrast to those who reduced analysis to one aspect such as characterisation, technique, or some historical context. In particular he objected to those who by studying minor writers attempt to define the probable Shakespeare world view. It is easy to see Knight's limitations. He had no interest in historical, political or social context. His theory of organic form belongs to the nineteenth century. But when all is said and done, Knight understands the imaginative nature of literature in contrast to Caroline Spurgeon (1935), for example, who assumes that lists of images tell us about Shakespeare himself.

Knight claims that in *Coriolanus* War and Love are in opposition. While War in the play signifies power, ambition, nobility and efficiency, nearly all the positive qualities of life, it ignores Love. Because of this war becomes contradictory, self-poisoning, as will any value that does not include love. Knight comments that the style is bare and that we are in a world of civil strife, quarrels over grain and corn, hard weapons, the contact of battle. There is little light, little colour; life seems provincial, limited, with war the only relief. The imagery is metallic. Even the fishes 'swim with fins of lead' [I.i.182]. We hear of 'leaden spoons, Irons of a doit' [I.v.5–6]. (It is a fault of Knight's way of arguing and the selectivity of his approach to spatial patterns that he ignores the contrasting 'cushions' in the same speech.) Another pattern of related images concerns architecture and building, images of a state built on hardness. 'Such references often derived from the essentially "civic" setting. And the present civilization is clearly a hard one, a matter of brick and mortar, metals and stones.' Knight develops a contrast to *Antony and Cleopatra*. There civilisation catches fire, harvests are rich, people form friendships. Here in Rome the city walls limit, the world is constricted. 'Hostile cities are here ringed as with the iron walls of war, inimical, deadly to each other, self-contained.' (Knight works by contrasts, his generalisations are based on details, images, from the text; the generalisations are argued from an imaginative entering into the text, so that city, hero, commercial norms seem one, not opposed as in most readings.) 'Thus our city imagery blends with war imagery, which is also "hard" and metallic. And that itself is fused with the theme of Coriolanus' iron-hearted pride.' In Menenius' speech we can see the associations of building with Coriolanus' hardness of spirit:

MENENIUS.    See you yond coign o'th'Capitol, yond corner-
       stone:
SICINIUS.    Why, what of that?

MENENIUS.   If it be possible for you to displace it with your
little finger, there is some hope ladies of Rome, especially
his mother, may prevail with him.   [v.iv.1–6]

In *Coriolanus* there is no romance of war; none of the
attractions Othello or Antony have as famous conquerors.
The play is not even filled with horror and 'portentous'
warnings. Coriolanus and others fight, break through city
walls, are violent, bloody, harsh, clamorous: 'make you ready
your stiff bats and clubs' [i.i.161]. That is Rome. In Antium
Coriolanus worries that 'thy wives with spits and boys with
stones In puny battle slay me.' A serving man says 'This
peace is nothing but to rust iron, increase tailors, and breed
ballad-makers' [iv.v.230–1]. We hear of weapons, hardness,
violence, impact. When Aufidius and Coriolanus demonstrate
their mutual admiration and loyalty to the code of warriors:

> Let me twine
> Mine arms about that body, where against
> My grained ash an hundred times hath broke
> And scarred the moon with splinters. Here I clip
> The anvil of my sword. . . .
>                                         [iv.v.110–14]

Although it might have helped his structural contrasts,
Knight is one-sided in his selection of images. The speech
goes on to refer to the hot, noble love of the two warriors for
each other. Instead Knight again picks up images of violence.
He notes suggestions of infinity in the warrior images ('And
scarr'd the moon'), the images of blood and the emphasis on
violence. 'Here human ambition attains its height by splitting
an opponent's body.' Analysing the Cominius description of
Coriolanus' valour in ii.ii.109–24, Knight says:

> Notice the metallic suggestion: the city 'gate', 'din' which 'pierces' his
> sense, the fine hyperbole of Coriolanus 'striking' the whole town with
> planetary impact. All this blended with 'blood' – he is 'a thing of blood',
> 'painting' Corioli with its people's blood, himself 'reeking'. There is, too,
> 'death'. His sword is 'death's stamp', he runs over 'the lives of men',
> and dying cries punctuate his advance. Iron, blood, death. But the price

of this excessive and exclusive virtue is that Coriolanus becomes a blind mechanism, ruthless as death itself.

Knight shifts from focusing on images to constructing a character and psychology which will explain the narrative. 'His wars are not for Rome; they are an end in themselves. Therefore his renegade attack on Rome is not strange. His course obeys no direction but its own; he is a power used in the service of power.' He is 'a blind mechanic, metallic thing of pride and pride's destiny'.

Such an interpretation is reinforced by sound patterns: 'a violent and startling polysyllable set amid humble companions', 'two thunderous words in one line', 'strange polysyllables' such as conspectuities [II.i.66], empiricutic [II.i.122], cicatrices [II.i.156], carbonado [IV.v.195]. Such words and sounds reflect the whole play where Coriolanus strides gigantically, thunderously above the multitude.

The nature imagery is usually in pairs of strong weak, suggestive of the inborn inequality of Coriolanus and others: osprey fish, eagle dove, lions and hares, foxes and geese, oaks and rushes, boy and butterfly, eagles and crows, cat and mouse. Such images prepare for the victory of love while showing the natural excellence of the hero. At the climax Volumnia is strong because she 'pits his filial love against his pride'; love is a force of nature stronger than others:

> What's this?
> Your knees to me? To your corrected son?
> Then let the pebbles on the hungry beach
> Fillip the stars; then let the mutinous winds
> Strike the proud cedars 'gainst the fiery sun,
> Murdering impossibility, to make
> What cannot be, slight work!
> [v.iii.56–62]

Through imagery we examine character and psychology. Coriolanus' pride and virtue are twined and intrinsic to each other. They are dedicated to honour as a good in itself. As he fights for honour's sake, not Rome, honour became disassociated from love. That is why Coriolanus insults others using

images of curs, rats, scabs. His few patriotic phrases sound
trite, hollow, glib; he is dearer to himself than is Rome. His
moments of sympathy with other soldiers are exceptional;
he is an automaton concerned with war and honour. His
relationship with Aufidius shows him in a true light. (Because
Knight is still stuck with a Bradleyian concept of character
he does not allow for contradictions.)

Knight then turns to Volumnia 'the iron mother of an iron
son. She has no interests, no sympathy, no understanding,
save in one direction: her son's honour.' This is a play of irony
as well as iron. She loves to picture Coriolanus bloody,
embattled, scorning others, fighting for her. But she will cause
his death.

Knight examines the disease imagery and suggests that in
terms of the body politic metaphor, Coriolanus, not the
citizens, is the disease which must be cast out. He is the
irritant which provokes anger and civil war. As he becomes
monstrously mechanical killer, or dragon, he lacks mercy and
love. He is power, valour, pursuing its own course. Neither
he nor his mother have shown any real love; they have
been concerned with honour. Love is impossible without
community. As mother and son follow their own pride in
seeking honour they find themselves facing each other as
opponents, she for Rome, he for himself. 'No Shakespearean
play drives its protagonists to so bitterly an ironic climax.'
Faced by mother, wife and child, the love he repressed proves
stronger than he expected. Coriolanus cannot be author of
himself. Examining the imagery of the meeting between
Coriolanus and his family in Act v.iii Knight shows its lyricism,
and softness which dissolves 'the metal of his fierceness'. In
Volumnia, Virgilia and Valeria, Coriolanus' pride is 'opposed
by three forms of feminine beauty: motherhood, wifehood,
maidenhood'. Love is found after all to rule the world. 'Now
as Rome celebrates, we find images of music and the sun
dances.' Coriolanus, however, must be sacrificed 'that communities may remain in health'. Knight's criticism has an
anthropological side; he shares with T. S. Eliot and Kenneth
Burke assumptions of common myths and rituals which are
the substructures of social and dramatic forms.

Knight gives a surprising reading to the end of *Coriolanus* which he finds triumphant. Allowing himself to be conquered by love Coriolanus has been purified. He could not have lived uprooted from community; through love he earns our sympathy and has a new source of pride. By sacrificing honour to love he for the first time can boast 'with reckless joy'. His speeches in Corioli, which many critics regard as an attempt to cover up a disaster or even suicidal, Knight sees as a liberation. Though vanquished Coriolanus triumphs, 'infinity now aureoles' him: 'his fame folds in / The orb o'th'earth' [v.vi.125–6]; he is in his splendour, 'Alone I did it' [v.vi.116].

This is an interesting reading, original, and along with Bradley is the basis of most future discussion of the play; but it is a selective, limited consideration of evidence. Knight's patterns seem to overwhelm the evidence; his imagination rather than Shakespeare's might be the text. Patterns of theme and image are superior over characterisation and other approaches which depend on narrative so long as the critic sticks to patterns and does not try to fill in the gaps, cover over ambiguities and contradictions. Knight becomes unsatisfactory when he tries to tidy up events and images into a tight package, a package which requires consistency of character, emotion, dramatic argument; such consistency returns us to pre-modernism, to classical rationality. There seems to be a lesson; avoid tidiness. Let the work explain itself. Having accepted that spatiality is itself a means of organisation do not impose moral or psychological structures on the events.

*The slide from imagery to moral judgement and narrative*

L. C. Knights follows on from G. Wilson Knight but is more conservative in approach as he relies more on characterisation, narrative and moral judgement. The Foreword and opening chapters to *Some Shakespearean Themes* (1960) claim that Shakespeare's plays form a coherent whole, express an evolving attitude towards life and that the essential structure of the plays is rather to be found in their poetic drama than in plot or character. The verse is the centre of the vitality of the plays, or how we respond to the plays, and the verse not only is a

clue to the themes associated with the characters but shapes
the figures in the carpet, the themes or attitudes in the canon
as a whole. Imagery is the basis of interpretation; when the
reader is awakened to significances deeper than plot and
character the plays seem living structures of recurring and
inter-related imagery. Knights, however, brings moral judgement to bear on what is revealed by a reading of themes and
images. Where Wilson Knight wants life and love L. C.
Knights shares some of Bradley's commonsense moralism.
'There is also the tragedy of the divided and mutilated city;
and a fundamental insight that what this play embodies is
that political and social forms cannot be separated from, are
in fact judged by, the human and moral qualities that shape
them, and the human and moral qualities that they foster.'
This insistence on moral judgement distinguishes Knights and
Leavis, and other *Scrutiny* critics, from Wilson Knight.

Traversi is another critic influenced by Wilson Knight who
finds it difficult to stay with imagery. In *An Approach to
Shakespeare* (1969) Traversi recalls Knight when noting that
the imagery of *Coriolanus* is 'rigid and unadorned, more
appropriate to a village or a country town than to a capital
of historical significance'. The society is faced by a 'struggle
for power in a world once restricted and pitiless'. Commenting
upon Menenius' parable Traversi says 'images of food and
digestion answer to the real state of the Roman polity.
Stagnation and mutual distrust, mirroring the ruthlessness of
contrary appetites for power, are the principal images by
which we are introduced to the public issues of *Coriolanus*.'
This is excellent criticism as is the identification of heroism
and glory with a cult of masculinity. Volumnia's description
of her grandson having 'mammocked' a butterfly is 'comment
on the deadly lack of feeling which has surrounded' Coriolanus
from birth and which he shares. Coriolanus is both a hero
and a childish undeveloped human being. While Traversi
continues to quote a few images, he drifts back into characterisation, psychology and narrative. Coriolanus' 'true enemy lies
finally, not in those around him, but in himself'. 'The
demagogic demands of the tribunes are balanced by an
unreasoning obstinacy in the warrior.' When Coriolanus,
faced by his mother's pleading, attempts to smother his

instincts, he is renegade to 'his own being' as well as his family
and city.

## Visual imagery

Charney (1961) notes in *Coriolanus* little figurative language
of fancy; when Coriolanus uses figurative language he prefers
simple similes rather than metaphors. Such similes add
vividness of force rather than convey new areas of significance.
The style of the play reflects Coriolanus' attitude towards
speech. He has an aversion to words as they represent flattery,
eloquence, politics; for him an inability to speak is 'a claim
to integrity'. The style of *Coriolanus* is not so much 'Roman'
as 'objective and public'. If the verbal imagery is disappoint-
ing, the play is filled with visual imagery as, for example,
when we see Coriolanus standing in his robe of humility, or
the way the yielding of Coriolanus to his mother's plea is
shown by the stage direction '*He holds her by the hand*'. Except
for kissing Virgilia, 'this is the only physical contact between
Coriolanus and another human being in the entire play, and
it indicates a climactic moment of reconciliation.'

## Religious, sociological and anthropological approaches

In Shakespeare's plays there is usually some religious allegory
or some Christian dimension which is applied if only intermit-
tently to the narrative, usually towards the conclusion. The
usurpation of Richard II, God's representative on earth,
unleashes a long period of political instability and civil war,
a national curse. Shakespeare may or may not have believed
this explained the wars between the houses of York and
Lancaster as secular explanations are given as well; but the
religious vision is there as a perspective which allows the plays
to be read as a homily on the need to obey divinely approved
monarchy. Hamlet faces a conflict between the secular and
the religious, and learns to resign himself to divine providence.
Some of Shakespeare's characters' suffering and sacrifice may
recall Christ's passion and death. Some plays, such as *Measure*

*for Measure*, are capable of being fully allegorised as we become aware of biblical echoes, allusions, parallels and symbols.

Simmons (1973) claims there is an unspoken ironic contrast in *Coriolanus* between Roman virtue and Christian love. Roman virtue as defined by Plutarch was 'valiantness'. 'Now in those dayes, valiantnes was honoured in Rome above all other vertues: which they call *virtus*, by the name of vertue it selfe, as including in that all name, all other special vertues besides. So that *virtus* in the Latin, was as much as valiantnesse.' (The 1595 version of Plutarch's 'Life of Ceisi Martius Coriolanus'.) Coriolanus embodies such virtue to the extreme and has been raised in it by his mother. Others assume that such virtue will be put to the use of Rome, but the election to the consularship and the creation of the new office of tribunes sullies the notion of pure virtue; they demand that other currencies – popularity, willingness to court the people, love of others – be used to pay for honour rather than honour being 'valiantness'. Coriolanus' notion of honour is independent of public payment, whether by the spoils of war or by office, and is therefore dirtied by the demand that he be political, accommodating, ingratiating, elected. Viewed in other ways we may say Coriolanus is being adolescent, acting from class prejudices, or has sexual fears of contamination, but within the perspective that Simmons examines, a perspective which is unquestionably in the play, Coriolanus pursues a notion of virtue with a purity beyond that of the other characters. The pursuit of Roman virtue brings him into conflict with the flawed Rome he serves, exiles him, and, ironically, appears only to find possible fulfilment in his valiantness in destroying Rome. Roman virtue thus turns against itself. It is an impossible ideal of virtue.

Simmons assumes that 'in his Roman tragedies Shakespeare is at one and the same time recreating the historical reality of the glory that was Rome and perceiving that reality in a Christian perspective.' Although the Roman heroes can only play their parts within their vision of the world, the reader, supposedly, is aware of the limitations of the vision and sees the events through a Christian perspective. The Rome of the play is set within the vision of St Augustine's *The City of God* where the earthly city is contrasted to the Heavenly City. This is a flawed contextual reading in which it is assumed that some position shapes the creation of the work of art and can be used to interpret its details.

Simmons' argument is methodologically weak since *Coriolanus* offers few biblical echoes or Christian symbols and the argument can only be sustained by the claim that the lack of such evidence is proof of the need for an ironic vision of events. Coriolanus' refusal to show his wounds can be seen as part of 'typological parody of the reverence and love behind Christ's stigmata and open hands'. Simmons argues the Third Citizen's 'we are to put our tongues into those wounds and speak for them', and other wound-mouth-tongue imagery implies 'a ritual in which the outward sign transubstantiates the inner grace. This action, in which the hero must show his wounds in the spirit of humility and self-sacrifice, begs with tragic operative irony the blessed "other case" – mankind's accepting, and therefore participating in, the benefits of Christ's Passion.'

There is one passage in *Coriolanus* which has sometimes been suggested as Christ-like: when his mother convinces him not to sack Rome, Coriolanus foresees his death as a result of making peace. His 'let it come' might be viewed as Christ's acceptance of his destiny to die to reconcile man with God. While the text must be pressed hard [v.iii.187–91] to carry the significance, supporting evidence is the theme of mercy which appears towards the end of the play. 'He wants nothing of a god but . . . mercy' [v.iv.24–6]; 'thy mercy and thy honour' [v.iii.200].

By arguing for irony (the saying of the opposite) Simmons has allegorised the play. Like a biblical interpreter he uses scraps of evidence as proof of a theological doctrine which supposedly has shaped the narrative and which the story is said in some way to illustrate. This is no different from a Marxist interpretation or any interpretation which reads a work of art as a metaphoric extension of some master trope or supreme fiction – Christianity, Marxism, The White Goddess, or Progress. At his worst Simmons' offers improbable allegorisations, such as interpreting *Coriolanus* in terms of John Calvin's *Commentaries on the Book of the Prophet Daniel*: Shakespeare's imagery of iron, dragons, and love between men is explained as deriving from the Bible and explicated

with reference to Calvin's marginalia. If such excesses of
scholarship and Christian allegorising make Simmons' readings appear special pleading he shows why the Roman plays
seem so futile; a pagan world in which action can only
be referred to secular social norms lacks purpose and is
disillusioning. There is no suggestion of a dimension that
would give life purpose, meaning, consolation. While the plays
with Christian dimensions may show a futile secular world
there are symbolic patterns which offer consolation – confession, repentance, restoration and an afterlife. There is in
*Coriolanus* a Roman concept of the city as a mother, the city
as in itself the ground or ultimate end of activity; but
Shakespeare does not recreate a Roman mythology as an
alternative dimension to Christianity. There are allusions to
Mars, Diana and other classical gods, but they offer no
coherent picture of a cosmos. When, however, Coriolanus
seeking revenge is referred to as god-like, a view of the cosmos
is implied. The gods seem all-powerful, but without care, pity
or mercy for humanity.

### Coriolanus as sacrificial scapegoat

From an anthropological standpoint communal ritual is the
foundation of religion. If we see Coriolanus as a sacrificial
figure it might better explain his function in the play than by
transforming him into an ironic Christ. Burke (1966) assumes
that tragedy is a secularisation of ancient ritual; a tragic play
should have at its core 'some kind of symbolic action in which
some notable form of victimage is imitated, for purgation, or
edification of an audience'. The character or hero must be
suitable to be a sacrificial victim and the situation or plot
must be plausible in such a way that the audience will accept
(and participate in) the 'victimage'. The symbolic dimension
in the play will be relevant both to the topics or themes of the
play and to the society for which the play has been made.

*The class struggle*

Burke sees Shakespeare projecting social problems from the London of his day on to ancient Rome. This creates an acceptable 'distance'. He assumes that *Coriolanus* has behind it the suffering of the poor as a result of the Enclosure Acts which dispossessed many tenants from the land and he refers to the riots which others sometimes see as the topical source of the plays; he sees an analogy between the plebeians of Rome and the under-privileged of England, and between the patricians and the privileged; he assumes conflict between the haves and the have nots. Coriolanus as hero dramatises this conflict; his pride as warrior and his belief in the rights of his class bring out conflict rather than glossing over it the way Menenius does. From his first entrance on stage Coriolanus heightens class conflict. He is excessively proud, excessively truthful, excessively representative of the values which Rome thought necessary for virtue. There is no temperance, no middle way for Coriolanus. His virtues and vices are similar and make him a potentially tragic figure, a sacrifice to relieve social tensions. Like Cordelia, another tragic sacrificial figure, he cannot speak well, he cannot pretend. He therefore cannot be accommodated in a complex society with its division of labour since he brings out the divisiveness which is part of the social system. His death following the raising of tension is cathartic.

Ritual has a function within society; ritual is a structure or gesture, to use Burkean terminology, which might have various purposes but here has a psychological-sociological content. In particular, Burke suggests that the possible context is a period when 'many *nouveaux-riches* were being knighted . . . it is *new* fortunes that people particularly resent'. He sees the social context as part of a change from feudal to class factionalism; a transvaluation has taken place from the religious to nationalism and with this there is a new kind of factionalism, the class struggle. However, various kinds of motivation are present in the play: the family factionalism that was part of feudal relations, the class motivation that is part of the new national order, the motivation of nationalism and individualism. Burke does not claim individualism is a unique post-medieval system;

rather he sees individualism as universal. We are biologically individuals. In most societies, the individual has a sense of himself, a name, private pains. Individual-family-class-nation are tangled and become knotted when Coriolanus, the individual, sees himself as part of a family which is part of a class which in his mind is the nation. He is manoeuvred by his mother, the patricians, and the tribunes into a position where he in revenge is going to attack the nation. The situation has become grotesque, how does it contribute to the medicinal?

### Coriolanus as satyr

Here Burke has a brilliant insight. Coriolanus is like a figure from a satyr play who rails at and lampoons others. From his first appearance on stage, he is a master of vituperation; he stirs up the political system and keeps the play active. Unlike Timon of Athens, Coriolanus is disrespectful and scurrilous to the plebeians only, not to the patricians. His rages are infantile. His is a child's invective; it is the rage of those who are powerless. Whether or not we agree with his views we take pleasure in expressing what is socially repressed. Coriolanus provides an outlet, an outlet which while medicinal is also dangerous. Coriolanus' suitability for the role of scapegoat is his excessiveness, the way he brings out the conflicts between self, family, class and nation. His excesses, while purging our repressions, are punished, and thus a promise of general peace. Burke's title is 'Coriolanus – and the Delights of Faction'.

Burke's study of Coriolanus is brilliant in its fullness of vision and analysis of many different but related kinds of behaviour. The scapegoat ritual has a different social dimension in the modern world of the nation state and within a society organised by classes. The curious richness of motivation in the play shows differing kinds of society – feudal notions of family loyalty sitting alongside class notions and loyalty to state. Coriolanus' railing and insults bring social tensions to a head and make him the focus for resentment – a figure whose death will be felt as cathartic. He speaks the resentments of his class towards the lower orders. As he is resented by those he insults, his death is a promise of reconciliation between classes, between family and state. Individualism is seen as biological, not a social construct; it is therefore likely to be in conflict with family, class and state. The play ennobles the individual while sacrificing him to larger social groups.

Burke's theoretical approach anticipates yet is fuller and more satisfying than that of recent theorists. Its weakness is a lack of relationship to details of the text and to a specific context. Why is this a period of the *nouveaux riche*? Is Coriolanus really motivated by feudal family values rather than by his dependency on his mother? Burke's ideas have some of the inclusiveness and therefore unprovableness of comment about the rise of the middle class. If the death of Coriolanus is medicinal why do so many critics record a sense of futility at the end? Comprehensive theorisation bringing in many realms of human activity is desirable, but the study of literature also needs the concreteness of, say, Brecht's analysis of the first scene of *Coriolanus* and a demonstratable relationship between an art object, social group, ideology and historical context.

### History as the absurd: Coriolanus in Eastern Europe

The assumption that *Coriolanus* is about class warfare informs much criticism of the play. Kott (1964) looks at the class struggle and historical developments in the play from the perspective of a disillusioned Marxist, someone who had seen the Communist Party as the main barrier against the triumph of Fascism and as the liberator of Eastern Europe. Subsequently the Russian occupation of Poland and Stalinism leads to loss of faith in the notion that history is evolving towards some better future. Instead of the death of God, Kott's view is shaped by the death of purposeful History. There is a process, the process is perhaps predictable, but the results are cruel, disillusioning. Kott offers an Eastern European, post-Marxist vision of The Absurd. The Absurd results from incongruity, or what Kott calls contradictions. Instead of Marxist contradictions working themselves out into a dialectic of progress, there is a grotesque dialectic of mean, brutal, unsatisfying change. Kott praises Shakespeare for offering a realistic view of history as purposeless, absurd, rather than as a comfortable ideology. Thus Shakespeare becomes our contemporary.

Unlike many critics who only treat *Coriolanus* as a struggle between the hero and the people, Kott discusses the second half of the play after the banishment. The first half has 'a republican moral'. An ambitious general who despises the people aims at dictatorial power, is banished and betrays his country by going over to the enemy. The second half of the play has a contradictory message. Having driven out its military leadership the city has no defence and is 'doomed to destruction'. The people 'can only hate and bite', but are unable to defend their city. Among the nameless crowd 'only Coriolanus was a great man. . . . History is cruel and abounds in traps. The great ones fall, the little ones remain.' Shakespeare in *Julius Caesar* and *Coriolanus* has introduced Republican Rome into tragedy, and history has now become ironic. Coriolanus is marked by greatness but is crushed by history. The play reveals a bitter, pessimistic, cruel philosophy of history.

Kott sees three basic notions of society in the play. Two are of classes; the plebeians hold an egalitarian version of it. Coriolanus holds a hierarchical view. The third notion is that of solidarity, the organic body metaphor used by Menenius. Each contains a vision of how society should be organised, each is a reflection (an ideology) of the group or person using it, and each proposes to explain or organise the world. Shakespeare holds the three systems – egalitarian, solidarity and hierarchic – to criticism, confronting them by history. The war with the Volscians is the first contradiction, making egalitarianism foolish. The plebeians act like rats, are only interested in looting the dead. Hierarchy seems proved as the way of history. But even in victory there are reminders of the cost. Titus Lartius in Corioli is 'Condemning some to death, and some to exile.' When his wife weeps Coriolanus reminds her and us that 'Such eyes the widows in Corioles wear and mothers that lack sons.' History consists of losers as well as victors. Cruelty is required by such an heroic, hierarchical society. However, by an irony of history Rome has now become 'the people'. Sicinius says 'What is the city but the people?' and the Citizens reply 'The people are the city'. Once the consciousness of the people has entered history it may be repressed but it cannot be driven out. From now on such values as patriotism and public fame must co-exist with those of egalitarianism. Regardless of being stupid or stinking, 'the people are Rome, and Coriolanus is a traitor to his country'.

Where can Coriolanus go? The world is not empty. He will be a revenger, a Tamburlaine, a scourge who will cleanse the city by destroying it. But the days of divine scourges are over. This is not a play of divine providence. History 'has caught' Coriolanus 'and driven him into a blind alley; has made a double traitor of him'. He will betray his country and then betray himself and his own sense of himself by giving in to his mother's pleas. Kott, like Burke, finds a sublime, absurd but not to be despised, individualism in Coriolanus after his banishment. Kott sees in Coriolanus' god-like inhumanity, in his dismissal of his former friends and loves, a wish to destroy an unsatisfactory, contradictory world. 'Coriolanus opposes the world with his own absurd system of values.' The patricians, with their ideology of social solidarity (in which they are the favoured stomach) and the plebeians have demanded compromise from Coriolanus and by trying to accept such demands he has been destroyed. Now at the end of the play when he appears to rise once more and become 'an avenging deity' he finds himself again defeated by history. He has become a traitor and must now perjure himself to the Volscians if he is to get out of the role of avenger. He must be false to himself to be true to himself as a Roman noble. To save Rome is to destroy himself. Coriolanus suffers an ignoble death and, ironically, is then praised by the man who plotted against and killed him, the one warrior whom he respected as an equal. Kott says that *Coriolanus* is not popular as a play since it offers no solution to the contradictions of history, no shared system of values for the city or state and the individual. The fact that one does not love the people is not reason enough to be declared the enemy of the people; that is the real bitter drama of humanism.

*False analogies and lack of psychology*

Such a brilliant essay is persuasive rather than convincing. What is to stop Coriolanus and his friends from repressing the plebeians? Why assume that class only came into being with the early modern period? There is also the avoidance of psychology. How can we understand why Coriolanus does not destroy Rome without discussing his relationship to his family and especially to his mother? Coriolanus cries when rejected by his mother. The text several times mentions it: 'it is no little thing to make / Mine eyes to sweat compassion' [v.iv.195–6], 'At a few drops of women's rheum . . . he sold the blood and labour / Of our great action' [IV.v.436–48], 'For certain drops of salt' [v.vi.93], 'at his nurse's tears / He whined' [v.vi.97–8], 'thou boy of tears:' [v.vi.101]. Coriolanus' relationship to his mother ironically fulfils what the tribunes earlier say about him. They seem to know him better than we may at first be willing to accept in the light of their mean-spirited attitudes. Another issue that Kott and Burke avoid is how Volumnia persuades Coriolanus to change his mind. Exactly what does she say, what is effective?

Attempting to avoid the self-determinacy of Marxist history, Kott has created an absurdist version in which history determines itself without any purpose. He allegorises *Coriolanus* into a version of Polish twentieth-century history. The way Kott's essay on *Coriolanus* concludes, celebrating the individual as victim of the people, seems strangely romantic. It signifies more than it says, and I suspect what it means has much more to do with Kott's Poland than with what we both might agree to find in Shakespeare's play. In my 'reading' or interpretation of Kott's criticism, his *Coriolanus* seems a metaphor for Stalinism, for the Leninist idea of the party as vanguard. If I ask myself about the hero who defends the state but who is trapped by the corridors of history, I recall the Polish old order, the aristocracy.

Those who see *Coriolanus* as a metaphor of a class struggle too often rapidly move away from the text. When Kott refers to anything with a direct bearing on the play it stands out as having a different, stronger interest. He mentions in passing that Livy's version of the history of Coriolanus has a different conclusion from the Plutarchan version Shakespeare uses. According to Livy Coriolanus retired peacefully and lived long afterwards among the Volscians. That Shakespeare ignored this story and chose a more bloody, cynical version tells me more about the imagination which shapes the play than most criticism.

*Social anthropology*

Every clan, tribe, society, nation has means of binding its members into believing they can only be human if they belong to it and that others are inferior: every society makes unreasonable demands on the individual. What is this society that uses, abuses, and finally brings about the death of Coriolanus? Paster (1985) discusses the conflict between the notion of the city as a means towards individual perfection and the reality in which 'perfection comes only through death'. 'The social mandate for heroic self sacrifice collides with the heroic mandate for self-realization conceived in civic terms.' Roman politics are predatory, savage, and destroy the hero.

In *Julius Caesar* and *Coriolanus* Shakespeare shows a real city; in each the governing order is challenged and the city is in crisis. The plays are concerned with the question of what a city is or should be. The patricians identify Rome with themselves; the tribunes see the city as its citizens. In the play as a whole 'Rome' occurs 86 times but almost always by the patricians. The tribunes use it six times; the citizens never. Identification with the notion of Rome is therefore patrician, although the idea of the city is claimed for the citizens. Rome is a patrician standard of conduct, an idea of how to behave, a concept of greatness which, as is shown by the plebs in battle, the poor do not share. Since the idea of Rome, of contributing to its greatness, works against including the plebs, they become outsiders, the opposing, despised Other. Coriolanus, who believes the ideology of his class, wants to rid Rome of the citizens as if 'they were barbarians'. They are less than human: 'Though in Rome litter'd; not Romans'. Romanness also means the civic obligation to sacrifice family to the honour and protection of the state. There is a conflict between the notion of equality of patricians and the fame and honour they seek. Within the communality not all patricians are equal. The more successful you are at being a Roman the more you threaten the balance of the state.

Food is an image of unity. In *Coriolanus* cannibalism, eating, feeding, are recurring images. The plebs are starving and demand cheap grain; this is granted by the patricians rather than risk revolt. Coriolanus would refuse the plebs cheap grain; they should fight the Volsces to take their grain. You only join Coriolanus' community as a soldier. But Rome devours its heroic sons to purge the city of its tensions. If Rome is identified with monuments, buildings, roofs, walls, the life of the city is associated in the imagery with animals, eating, parts of the body, violence. The plebeians see Coriolanus as a dog; Aufidus says Coriolanus is to Rome 'as is the osprey to the fish, who takes it'. Coriolanus wants the plebs to be lions and fox in battle; but instead they are hare and geese. Menenius says they are a wolf and describes Coriolanus as a lamb. Coriolanus calls Rome a 'city of kites and crows'. People symbolically eat people. Battle, war, is usually associated with eating. Coriolanus sees war as a means 'to vent our musty superfluity'.

Volumnia has nourished Coriolanus to be a Roman 'Thy valiantness was mine; thou suck'st it from me'. He has been nourished to be sacrificed. The blood images in the play link with the food images: blood is family, wounds, the life one gives for others. The plebs want to see blood from the hero, that shows he has symbolically died for them. Coriolanus will not show his wounds; he has died for some other cause, not for them.

Volumnia saves Rome by becoming the 'embodiment of mother Rome'. To march on Rome is to march 'on thy mother's womb'. Having made Coriolanus choose between shedding the blood of his family or giving up his revenge Volumnia speaks of her self as 'thy dear mother' [v.iii.161], a 'poor hen' who 'clucked thee to the wars, and safely home'. As Paster says 'to march against Rome is to turn against the sources of his life'. The fame and honour he sought can only be achieved in Rome through Romans; he cannot be author of himself. Volumnia has become that Roman dam that eats its young. Coriolanus dies so that Rome can live. When he tells his mother he will die for compromising, she makes no comment. He loves her; she loves Rome. I had better quote Paster who offers a more feminine vision than I naturally would:

> Shakespeare cannot deprive Rome of its central importance. It is worth saving because the city as mother is the source of nuture, training, and ideals, the achievement of common humanity, and the seat of the heart's affections, which it is impious, unnatural, and perhaps impossible to deny.

Because of the nature of the city, fragile, made up of class conflicts, the fickleness of the populace, the inevitable conflict between its best and the rest, such harmony can only come about through an endless process of violence and regeneration, comedy and tragedy. The community goes on; 'in the endless tragic comic cycle of regeneration, devouring the heroes it nurtures and immortalizes because it is in its nature to do so'. Yet by surviving at the cost of Coriolanus 'it survives diminished, starved by such feeding'.

Paster shifts the class conflict from a Marxist vision of history to the social structure of cities and communities, as likely to be found in ancient Rome as the present; she approaches the structure as an anthropologist might. The community must sacrifice its best if it is to survive since community requires both harmonious egality and inharmonious achievement. For the sake of the harmony the hero, while necessary, must be sacrificed. The food metaphor points to the predatory nature of life and cannibalism as part of survival. Nurture, community are feminine, the mother, the continuity of birth and regeneration in contrast to the masculine warrior, achiever, individual, son.

## Interdisciplinary approaches

Many recent critical theories are basically interdisciplinary approaches to literature. While structuralism and deconstruction are textually oriented, they evolved from a theory of language which is seen as self-referential systems loosely linked to reality. Thus for both, and for most post-modernist theory, language or kinds of discourse is the focus of discussion, and literature is no longer culturally privileged. Cultural materialists (usually Marxists), feminist, Lacanian and other critical approaches are perhaps only different from other interdisciplinary approaches – such as literature and philosophy, literature and the Fine Arts – in that their methodologies dominate the text, bringing, as in contextual approaches, assumed meanings or attitudes to bear. They, and the deconstructionalists, would argue that other approaches are shaped by unrecognised ideologies, such as patriarchy, capitalism, liberalism, empiricism, etc., and conclusions are inscribed in the assumptions which shape the methods.

### Marxist

Older Marxists saw literature in relation to the class struggle over ownership of the means of production – the struggle to determine who distributes the social product. Such Marxist analysis was largely sociological; literary production and the themes of literature were understood directly in relation to class. Thus Burke and Kott assume *Coriolanus* portrays or reflects a class struggle although they seem to differ about who represents whom. Burke sees Coriolanus as having the pride and self-assertion of a rising class or newly rich whereas Kott seems to find him representative of some older order of individualism or perhaps even the last of the aristocrats overtaken by the working class. It is of interest that Burke and others, such as Eagleton, seem to detect behind the character of Coriolanus bourgeois individualism rather than a dying feudal order. This is curious as the most obvious way to read the play in socio-economic terms would be to regard Coriolanus as part of an older feudal order, the patricians, being challenged by new urban bourgeoisie of shop keepers, lawyers, traders, and other citizens. This is how Shakespeare's plays were understood by orthodox Russian Marxist critics such as A. A. Smirnov who claimed that Shakespeare criticised both social classes but was sympathetic to the citizens in *Coriolanus*.

*Post-structural Marxist*

The shift from older to new Marxist approaches came as a result of the fusion of Marxism with semiotics, structuralism, or other linguistically based theories of analysis. Instead of ideology being a kind of propaganda by which a class defends its values, a class remaking history, truth, nature and other values according to its own convenience, ideology now became encoded in the very structures by which we perceive and understand reality. Thus all vision has to be both ideological and part of some structure of language (using the term broadly to mean a system of signs). Various fusions of this kind dominate modern critical theory with the intent of the critic now being to unmask, demystify or show the operation of ideology in a text.

Eagleton (1986) begins by arguing that linguistic stability is a sign of social order, but as Shakespeare is highly productive of puns, metaphors, riddles and other word play which unsettles a stable language his creativity is at odds with his political ideology and the plays are 'devoted to figuring out strategies for resolving' this contradiction. Rather than focusing on class struggle Eagleton's interest is 'the interrelations of language, desire, law, money and the body' in Shakespeare's plays. Coriolanus is 'though literally a patrician, perhaps Shakespeare's most developed study of bourgeois individualist, those "new men" (for the most part villains in Shakespeare) who live "As if a man were author of himself and knew no other kin".' (In view of most psychological readings it is doubtful many will agree that 'Coriolanus is as superbly assured in his inward being as Hamlet is shattered in his'.) Linguistic theory seems to have replaced Volumnia when Eagleton claims 'Coriolanus confers value and meaning on himself in fine disregard for social opinion, acting as signifier and signified together'. 'Coriolanus is nothing *but* his actions, a circular, blindly persistent process of self-definition. He cannot imagine what it would be like not to be himself.' He is 'a kind of nothing . . . because he is exactly what he is, and so a sort of blank tautology' who will not 'engage in reciprocal exchange or submit to the signifier'. He looks forward to a time 'when a whole society will fall prey to the ideology of self-authorship, when all individuals will be only begetters of themselves, private entrepreneurs of their bodies and sole proprietors of a labour force.'

Eagleton's conclusions are inscribed in his method of analysis, including the assumption that one is shaped by society and its languge. Kott, living in Poland, has more sympathy with humanism; Eagleton welcomes a crisis in the individual and the supposed death of humanism brought about by linguistic theories – itself analoguous to the older Marxist view that people are created by social and historical situations. (One would have thought the expansion of inter-national capitalism, and the cultural relativism created by international communications were better, as well as more Marxist, explanations.) While Eagleton should believe in an economic base with all else superstructure, the precise relationship of the social and linguistic is confused since language becomes the way we conceptualise the historical and economic. His Marx seems rewritten by Borges.

## The decentring of man

Dollimore (1984) claims that whereas English and American literary criticism is aesthetically and ideologically obsessed with order many Renaissance writers were aware that ideology is embedded in social practices and institutions. The literature of the Jacobean period was sceptical, showed the collapse of the Elizabethan providential view of the cosmos and is characterised by discontinuity and the decentring of man similar to modern materialist analysis. Dollimore favours analysis which reveals that Christianity and Humanism are ideologies imposed on reality and not virtues. Coriolanus is for Dollimore, as for Eagleton, a prime example of the contradictions of bourgeois humanist essentialism. Coriolanus believes that his virtue is prior to and independent of his social environment. He feels superior by birth and by his actions regardless of what society may think. Volumnia, although educating him to such ideas, knows better; for her fame and reputation derive only from society and state. Where Coriolanus sees the world in terms of absolutes she understands that power is part of a social network 'in which intervention not essence is determining'. Dollimore argues '*Coriolanus* does not show the defeat of innate nobility by policy, but rather challenges the very idea of innate nobility. So when Coriolanus is exiled from Rome he declares confidently "There is a world elsewhere" [III.iii.137]. But it is the world being left which he needs, because it is there that his identity is located.' When Coriolanus arrives muffled to offer himself to Aufidius the latter fails to recognise Coriolanus even though they have many times fought each other. This shows that 'Aufidius loves not the man but the power he signifies; he puts a face to the name, not vice-versa.'

I think Dollimore is off the track here. The scene is meant to be dramatic. Aufidius does not admire Coriolanus as a Roman leader of armies; he admires and dreams of the power of the man Coriolanus who personally beats him in battle. Dollimore's mis-statement of the case is similar to many misreadings, Marxist and otherwise, which seem so antagonistic to Coriolanus that you would never know that he is shown in the play winning a battle alone by himself and that the tide of battle shifts in his favour whenever he appears. His soldiers love him.

As the nature of Dollimore's discourse has been created to unmask power relations in bourgeois society there is predictability in what is offered as insights. 'Essentialist egotism, far from being merely a subjective delusion, operates in this play as the ideological underpinning of class antagonism.' Coriolanus needs the plebeians as 'a class to exploit at home' and as 'objects of inferiority without which his superiority would be literally meaningless'. (Again this ignores what Coriolanus does, there is no evidence of his exploiting of the plebs unless Dollimore is referring to the price of grain; the situation he describes might better apply to the tribunes who need Coriolanus to oppose to have power themselves.) Dollimore's inaccuracies unfortunately undermine the possible insight he offers.

Dollimore's target is what he calls 'essentialist humanism'. Dollimore's hero is the Aufidius of the later part of the play whose speech 'So our virtues / Lie in th'interpretation of the time' shows that virtues are socially constructed. 'With the dissolution of the universal . . . a new kind of history is disclosed . . . its focus is unmistakable: state power, social conflict and the struggle between true and false discourses.' Shakespeare once more seems to be in full agreement with the ideology and practice of the critic; he really is our contemporary.

### Psychoanalytical

Some of the most interesting insights into *Coriolanus* have been offered by psychological and psychoanalytical approaches. The tradition from Freud onwards of reading Shakespeare's plays as if they were open to psychoanalysis was continued by Hofling's (1957) 'An Interpretation of Shakespeare's *Coriolanus*' as a phallic narcissitic character whose narcissism expresses itself in an exaggerated display of self-confidence, superiority, and aggressive courage. He sees Coriolanus' personality formed by his mother, 'an extremely unfeminine, non-maternal person', who tried to mould her son to fit her own ideal of masculinity. Her method was to withhold praise and affection except for aggressive achievements. Not offered any emotional nourishment Coriolanus is filled with aggression exhibited through fierceness and his dislike of the plebeians and his attempted revenge on Rome. The later is interpreted as revenge on his mother. Viewed in this way, *Coriolanus* is a play about characters and their relations rather than politics.

Adelman's (1980) study of food imagery, dependency and aggression in *Coriolanus* builds upon previous studies to incorporate political and other considerations. Using the social context of enclosures and food riots Adelman claims that Shakespeare by beginning with the mutiny 'shapes his material from the start in order to exacerbate these fears in his audience'. If the portrait of hungry mouths demanding their own adds excitement to *Coriolanus* the centre of the play is 'the image of the mother who has not fed her children enough'. The social image is a projection of Volumnia's lack of nourishment of Coriolanus as a child. She has created her son by sending him to war 'at an age when a mother should not be willing to allow a son out of the protective maternal circle for an hour'. Blood and his wounds have become his nourishment rather than mother's milk. 'Thrust prematurely from dependence on his mother, forced to feed himself on his own anger, Coriolanus refuses to acknowledge any neediness or dependency'; he must view himself as totally self-sufficient. Praise threatens him as it implies that he is not self-sufficient and has acted to win approval of others. Asking, craving, desiring are the equivalent of eating; Coriolanus would rather starve than admit he wants or needs nourishment and is dependent on others. He wants to be author of himself, a self-creation symbolised by his new name, Coriolanus. His manhood is secure only when he plays the part Volumnia created for him. He must deny the possibility of changing, and refuses to assume different roles, such as flattering the public to become consul. He associates his manhood with being isolated, alone, independent from others. Deprived of nourishment, he seems to find it outrageous that others would not be and resents the demanding mob.

Shakespeare offers in the play a 'hungry world' in which everyone seems in danger of being eaten. Coriolanus is horrified by the mouth of the crowd which, a citizen says, wants to put tongues into his wounds. 'For the phallic exhibitionism of Coriolanus' life as a soldier has been designed to deny the possibility of kinship with the crowd; it has served to reassure him of his potency and his aggressive independence' and he fears collapse into infantile dependency. Having defined himself by opposition to the crowd Coriolanus constructs in Aufidius a likeness of himself, a mirror image of what he wants to be. Aufidius as invented by Coriolanus assures the latter of his 'own male grandeur'; thus he cannot see that Aufidius is a schemer and opportunist. His decision to go to Aufidius and their embrace is a 'flight from the world of Rome and his mother towards a safe male world'. Nourishment can be safely taken 'because it is given by a male'. Coriolanus' rage with Rome is really a hunger directed towards his mother. Rome has re-enacted the 'role of the mother who cast him out'. 'The cannibalistic mother who denies food and yet feeds on the victories of her sweet son stands at the darkest center of the play' as is shown by Menenius' remark about Rome being 'an unnatural dam' which eats 'her own'.

Adelman offers insight into the final scene between Coriolanus and his mother; Volumnia defeats her son by uncovering the defensive system he is using. His fantasies of revenging himself on her by killing her in the destruction of Rome are made explicit when she says she will kill herself and that he can only destroy Rome by treading on his own mother's womb. Her death would no longer be seen as an 'incidental consequence of his plan to burn Rome'. But as his notion of independence depends on the fantasy of being self-created, without kin, when this collapses he loses his defences.

Turning towards the distancing of the play Adelman notes that Coriolanus is as isolated from us as he is from everyone else; we never know what he is thinking. He dies as he has tried to live, alone. Coriolanus gives free expression to our desire to be independent but he also threatens us as we want him to be dependent and like us. If he is defeated by others we must give up our fantasy of omnipotence and independence, but the independence represented by the burning of Rome is intolerable. The kind of dependency shown in the play 'brings no rewards, no love, no sharing . . . it brings only the total collapse of the self'.

By concentrating on the psychological history of Coriolanus and his mother Adelman has provided a brilliant but limited character study. But the kind of approach limits and shapes what can be discussed. For all its brilliance the psychological approach seems unable at present to handle the openness, multiplicity and complexity of Shakespeare's plays.

## Theatre approaches: performance

In contrast to literary approaches there are interpretations of drama from the perspective of production, staging, acting, and so on. These include study of the theatrical mode or style of the period – a method I will discuss in Part Two – analysis of Shakespeare's staging, studies of actual performances and adaptations.

According to Berry (1981) performances of *Coriolanus* usually stress either the political aspect or character. In the late eighteenth–early nineteenth century John Philip Kemble strengthened Aufidius' jealousy of Coriolanus, and played the part of Coriolanus as 'a study in marble pride'. This interpretation Berry finds recurring over the past two centuries. The actor aims at loftiness, will, sternness, and austerity. Rigid pride earns an easy pseudo-Romanness while avoiding other issues in the play. By contrast Kean in the early nineteenth century avoided sublime contempt of the people and appeared more frustrated, raging, impotent, even childish. Being small rather than large Kean played to assert an identity. Macready's performances during the first four decades of the nineteenth century were marked by an increase in size of cast, a general expansiveness for the sake of spectacle. He made the mob on stage better dressed, better armed, confident rather than ill-dressed cowards. Possibly influenced by the reform movements of the nineteenth century, Macready sees the plebs as central figures opposed to Coriolanus. F. R. Benson's *Coriolanus* in 1901 gave even more vitality to the crowd and importance to the tribunes. Benson tried to soften the part of Coriolanus by playing him as boyish (the historical Coriolanus must have been in his mid-30s) and somewhat amusing. There was the famous French production of 1933–4 then understood as a right-wing, fascist denunciation of the supposed weakness and corruption of the socialist government. A 1952 Stratford production tried to separate warrior Coriolanus from the patrician to make him rather a tough soldier than a proud aristocrat. This Coriolanus is a likeable human if an aggressive military man. Laurence Olivier's 1959 *Coriolanus* at Stratford put emphasis on the relationship between the soldier and his rival rather than the conflict with the plebs. Private emotions, false modesty, sulky pride, narcissism, public-school self-belittlement, took priority over the fascist-communist interpretations of the 1930s.

Many recent interpretations are psychological rather than ideological. For a time, as in the John Neville–Tyrone Guthrie production of 1983, emphasis shifted towards homosexual feelings between Coriolanus and Aufidius. To view the play as private is radically different from most literary interpretations; literary critics see the play as public, mostly about politics. But acting traditions are different with identity, homosexuality and other private concerns as important as the political. The justifications for a homosexual reading are that Coriolanus is dominated by his mother; he seldom shows affection for his wife; he is chaste in exile and is as obsessed with Aufidius as Aufidius is with him. If physical contact between men in sports is regarded as latent homosexuality, fighting between two warriors carries this even further. Many productions feature a long embrace at ɪv.v.110–15; there are such revealing comparisons and remarks as Aufidius' claim that he is happier to see Coriolanus 'Than when I first my wedded mistress say / Bestride my threshold'. He dreams that he and Coriolanus are on the ground 'fisting each other's throat'.

In other productions Coriolanus is transformed into a class conscious anti-heroic aristocrat, a petty patrician, someone with an impossible code of honour who goes to pieces. He is varnish rather than a giant, upper-class correctness rather than a potential tyrant. Coriolanus also becomes part of a black-leather myth, the weak-strong boy who wants to be a man, the Roman in love with the foreign Volscians. Berry notes that while the 1970s was a period when British theatre was often political, *Coriolanus* had stopped being a political play on the British stage.

Productions of the play are significant in that various actors and directors put emphasis on psychological aspects that literary critics ignore. There is Coriolanus' possible acting of a role, his boyishness and domination by his mother, the psychology of his relationship with his mother, the psychology and latent homosexuality of his relationship and love–hate bond with Aufidius and what this may tell us about his unease in the civil-political world. In a play where everyone has an opinion of Coriolanus and where there is no one steady fixed perspective on him, why do literary critics accept his assertiveness on face value? Our obsession with equality blinds us to the possible subtexts of Coriolanus' character in the play. We do not see his weaknesses; yet directors find such subtexts and Shakespeare's method creates them.

The significance of performances is not limited to specific interpretations; that actors and directors can find such varied interpretations in each line shows the openness of the text, the possible multiplicity of meanings in the words. If each speech, each scene, every character can have a different, defendable interpretation, how is it possible to insist on one meaning having more authority than another? If readings are based on the discourse of previous interpretations, or on the conventions of contemporary art, or the concerns of our time, they apparently become a matter of preference not fact. The text remains the same but the methods of understanding, and the assumptions which shape them towards an interpretation, change. Put differently, *Coriolanus* is always there, but the nature of the reader changes.

Having taken interpretation of *Coriolanus* apart how can we put it together again? Or must we accept that post-modern criticism will be arbitrary, a deconstruction with no firm basis for reconstruction?

### *Transpositions*

The study of literature has in our time become a self-enclosed world with critic responding to critic. It is a corrective to see *Coriolanus* through the eyes of creative writers. Writers usually transform the play – the way Shakespeare transformed Plutarch – into a version of the tensions of their own age. Nahum Tate, John Dryden, John Dennis, Ibsen, T. S. Eliot, John Osborne, Arthur Miller, and Brecht, each finds in *Coriolanus* some combination of techniques or themes evolving in their own work. To read the play through the perspectives of later adaptations and styles is to see what a complex structure it has, a structure of thoughts, emotions, images, ideas, characters, events open to almost unlimited interpretations. The greatness is in its potentiality for significance.

Some dramatists read the play in the light of the politics of their time. According to Berry, Tate's *The Ingratitude of a Commonwealth or The Fall of Coriolanus* (1682) recommends 'Submission and Adherence to Establish Lawful Power' (during the Exclusion Crisis). John Dennis, after the Jacobite rebellion of 1715, wrote *The Invader of His Country, or The Fatal Resentment* (1719) with Coriolanus transformed into a Stuart pretender. As Dryden tried to move from the artificiality of the Heroic Play (with its epic plots, stylised dialogue and themes of love, honour, conquest) he wanted a drama which was affective and yet universalises. The bond between men of action, the mutual respect of two warriors, between Coriolanus and Aufidius, became an obvious model for Dryden's scenes of two warriors embracing in *All for Love*. Apparently he saw no homo-erotic implications in such mutual admiration. Rather he wanted to filter impurities from a type, and found in Shakespeare's play a partial model for the scenes in Act i, where Antony hugs Ventidius. Even more important was the meeting in Act v.iii with Volumnia; the pure emotionalism, the appeal to ties of family, to bonds between mother and son, wife and husband, child and father, is an influence on the scene in *All for Love*, Act iii, where Octavia leads Antony's two small daughters on stage and through an appeal to his emotions and honour, temporarily wins Antony back from Cleopatra. Similarly Dryden's hero, like Coriolanus, is a man of tears. In v.iii Coriolanus is conquered by his mother, the scene is highly emotionally charged. That the scene is one of deep emotion is pointed to (another trick Dryden learned from Shakespeare of the late tragic period) by 'But out, affection!/All bond and privilege of nature, break!' [v.iii.24–5]. The scene would have little purpose, and the irony that results would be ineffectual if it kept the same distance as elsewhere. The focus changes. The language itself points to the emotionality, 'those dove's eyes/Which can make gods forsworn? I melt, and am not/Of stronger earth than Mothers . . . Great Nature cries "Deny not"'. Dryden also learned such expressive rhetorical devices from *Coriolanus* as doubling exclamations and other charged phrases to point to emotion. When Coriolanus holds his mother by the hand he says 'O, mother, mother' and soon after 'O, my mother mother! O!' [v.iii.183–6].

It is useful to see *Coriolanus* through the eyes of Ibsen learning the art that built *A Doll's House*, an art which ensures irony, gaps, ambiguity, slippages, different perspectives. Those domestic realistic tragedies of the middle period are made up from short little scenes placed next to each other much the way Shakespeare constructs his plays. Ibsen's dramas gain their richness from juxtapositions, unexplained information, gaps in explanations, the tantalising subtexts which may or may not throw additional light on the main themes. Often we are given shreds of information about a character's past, which suggest another interpretation on the main action. The distancing, irony and subtexts are part of Shakespeare's method of construction. Ibsen found it particularly useful to demonstrate that what seems willed might be determined by the past (Nora and her father; Coriolanus and his mother).

In the opening scene of the play Coriolanus is described by the First Citizen as the 'chief enemy of the people' [1.i] Enemy of the people. The title of one of Ibsen's plays in which the hero becomes the outcast. In *An Enemy of the People* the chief character is a medical doctor who finds that a local factory has been polluting the water supply. This can result in typhoid. But as the town depends on tourists for its living its leaders, rather than close the baths for two years to improve the water supply, brand the doctor 'An enemy of the People'. The doctor's family suffers as a result. Ibsen has imaginatively transposed the characters and themes of Shakespeare's play to his own time; Coriolanus is now faced with the problems of industrialisation and the environment which conflict with supporting a family.

Ibsen shows that those who rule are self-seeking, ambitious and will harm the community through their decisions. The majority are found to be no better. The theme passed on through Ibsen to Arthur Miller; both those who govern and the majority refuse to face the truth. Instead of warning against Volsces, the modern Coriolanus warns against infections, pollution. Ibsen will return to this idea in *The Wild Duck* with the do-gooder's motives questioned. Does such honesty do as much harm as good? Does it reflect some private desire to triumph over or destroy others? The paradox that the person who is true to some higher code becomes the enemy of the people is directly in the situation of Shakespeare's play. The reversal that takes place between Coriolanus as patriot and standard of Roman virtue and the Coriolanus who is revenger, scourge of Rome, is like the do-gooder who, alienated from a corrupt society, interferes in the lives of others. The Coriolanus who is an archetype of Ibsen's heroes is a romantic individualist, an idealistic product of modern liberal notions of the self and its social duties.

In T. S. Eliot's two 'unfinished' Coriolan poems the hero

with 'no interrogation in his eyes' is contrasted to the common people who 'hardly knew ourselves' as they wait with stools and sausages. The Coriolan poems would appear to contrast the purposeful, cold hero (the indifferent sphinx of Yeats' 'Second Coming') to the purposelessness in modern life as represented by lack of religious faith and by the Statesman's endless, useless, time-wasting, time-consuming committees, rules, subcommittees. It is implied that Coriolanus belongs to some older, ritualistic past or belief. The proud Roman warrior, with his excess of one virtue, has become an 'enemy of the people' first as an Isbenite reformer, then as an Ibsenite troubled protestant do-gooder interfering in the lives of others. Eliot's Coriolanus is a symbol of undemocratic purposefulness and vitality in contrast to the modern age of industrialisation and mass culture. John Osborne rewrote the play under the title of *A Place Calling Itself Rome* where under the guise of Rome it becomes another *Look Back in Anger* at modern democratic England.

Such interpretations are as right or as wrong as most, being projections of contemporary concerns. What interests me is how Coriolanus changes from a romantic hero to a fascist leader. Marxist critics find nothing unusual about this since presumably the individualism of the past which gave birth to modern democratic ideas was bourgeois individualism and the play represents its inner contradictions. The history of ideas is a record of ideologies and their contradictions in relation to changing historical realities. The liberal-humanist critic, while not supporting Coriolanus' outbursts against the mob, is likely to be shocked that this possible symbol of romantic individualism has been condemned without just consideration for his services. We keep coming back to the fact that while Coriolanus represents what society values, society will not accept a leader who insists on disagreeable truths.

Arthur Miller's adaptation of Ibsen's *An Enemy of the People* tones down the anti-democratic sentiments in Ibsen's play. Ibsen finds amusement in Dr Stockmann's belief that the public will welcome his bringing of truth about the pollution of the water supply; he laughs at the comedy of the doctor expecting a testimonial instead being voted an enemy of the people (a reworking of Act III of *Coriolanus*). Miller, writing under the threat of McCarthyism and American pressure towards conformity, turns the play, as Martin Esslin notes, into 'a plea for the protection of unpopular minorities'. *Coriolanus* has been transformed into, to quote Miller, 'the question of whether one's vision of the truth ought to be a source of guilt at a time when the mass of men condemn it . . . there never was, nor will there ever be, an organized society able to countenance calmly the individual who insists that he is right while the vast majority is absolutely wrong.' But even Miller is unwilling to accept that Coriolanus' substitute, Dr Stockmann, might be superior to the masses because better educated, trained and more cultured as a result of being raised as an aristocrat. Miller deletes as 'fascist' Dr Stockmann's claim to superior knowledge resulting from superior culture. This reinterpretation of *Coriolanus* censors the possibility suggested by Ibsen that the elite might be better able to judge. The local newspaper owner and small shopkeeper of Ibsen's play are presented as no better than Shakespeare's citizens; they are ignorant through lack of education and influenced in their evaluation of the truth by economic considerations.

Brecht understood that the power of *Coriolanus* was in its fullness, its objective presentation of historical forces, even though they might contradict Shakespeare's own politics. Speaking of the way the 'plebeians' do not collapse after proclaiming their determination to revolt, Brecht notes that in Shakespeare they are not laughed off stage and indeed become united. Similarly he objects to claims that Menenius' fable of the body and the belly is not convincing; it is world famous and was the ideology of the time. Shakespeare gives the plebeians good arguments in reply. One of the actors comments about Coriolanus: 'It's interesting, this contempt for the plebeians combined with high regard for a national enemy, the patrician Aufidius. He's very class-conscious.' Another participant in the discussion comments on: 'The crystal clarity of Marcius's harangue! What an outsize character! And one who emerges as admirable while behaving in a way that I find beneath contempt!' Brecht replies:

And great and small conflicts all thrown on the scene at once: the unrest of the starving plebeians plus the war against their neighbours the

Volscians; the plebeians' hatred for Marcius, the people's enemy – plus his patriotism; the creation of the post of People's Tribune – plus Marcius's appointment to a leading role in the war. Well – how much of that do we see in the bouregois theatre.

This is excellent criticism. The generalisations are factual without becoming lost in detail and without being led away from the text by theory. The Marxist notion of literature as ideology and a reflection of class conflict strengthens the ability to describe the action and generalise about it; Brecht does not deny Coriolanus' grandeur or try to cut him down to size. Unlike some recent Marxist critics who argue that Shakespeare was the voice of the ruling powers and therefore must be demythified and deconstructed, Brecht's speakers examine the evidence:

> There's another point where Shakespeare refrains from coming down on the aristocratic side. Marcius isn't allowed to make anything of Plutarch's remark that 'The turbulent attitude of the base plebs did not go unobserved by the enemy'. He launched an attack and put the country to fire and sword.

Brecht recognised *Coriolanus* as having the objectivity he sought in his own epic theatre and that such fullness is lacking in modern drama.

# Part Two:
# Appraisal:
# Methodological
# Problems

IT IS USEFUL to review some of the advantages and
problems of various critical methodologies. Source and contextual studies assume that the background or context cited by
the scholar explains *Coriolanus*. If to avoid the crudeness of
direct influence we claim that an historical or other context
is mediated, we assign the significance of the play to a
generalisation or some untestable fiction of the past. If all
history is a fiction, being selective or creative narrative, how
can we situate *Coriolanus* in a context both specific enough to
be probable, yet mediated to avoid topical allegory associating
Coriolanus with Essex or Raleigh?

Just as proposed contexts create historical fictions, so
interpretation often returns to analysis of character, but
character is misleading in Shakespeare's plays as it is a
temptation to explain what is not explained or shown. Almost
every critic of *Coriolanus*, at some point, falls into characterisation as a means of explaining the story. Characterisation
soon leads to psychology. We need to be aware of its dangers
as fiction and that our perspective is either through the eyes
of other characters or through the eyes of the character. No
evidence is unprejudiced; character is not explainable on the
evidence presented. The story is also confused and full of gaps.
A successful form of interpretation of Shakespeare's plays has
been by way of imagery. Study of imagery assumes that spatial
structures of themes and symbol are as significant as character
or story. Most critics, however, are unable to keep to pure
study of structures of imagery and need to relate imagery to

story, character and, like most of those who discuss character, moral judgement. In interpreting any theatre analysis of stage craft and visual language is necessary.

*Coriolanus* is a play about a community as well as its main character. Some of the most interesting interpretations bring out such communal aspects as the class war, the ritualist basis of the hero's death, the social and political changes that require the hero's death. Rome seems a mediation for Jacobean England. That the play has no Christian dimension, makes it a study of the secular world. Shakespeare might have felt that secularity was the only world or he might have felt a world without religion was futile, but the play shows a predatory, dangerous world in which language is used as a weapon for persuasion and for disguise.

## Post-modernist theory or Jacobean theatre of mirrors?

We seem to have wandered into post-modern theory with our creation of unknowable characters, fictional contexts and self-referential art. This is to be expected. We read the art of the past according to the conventions of our time. The art that survives such changes in tastes becomes classic. Yet the conventions of the Globe Theatre plays, as explained by Beckerman (1962), are not that different from the post-modern. Beckerman's Renaissance theatre of multiplicity in which independent or semi-autonomous scenes mirror each other, and in which instead of classical unity there is an egalitarianism of plot, character, poetry and thoughts, sounds modernist. Of course it is not; it is of the Renaissance. According to Beckerman, the Globe plays – including *Coriolanus* – are not closely linked by cause and effect; the episodes contrast, echo, illustrate or in some way mirror each other. Each scene is a unit in itself, a unit in which the effect is often disproportionate to the cause. There is seldom a climax concentrated in one place; rather it is spread out or as in *Coriolanus*, multiplies (he is twice tried, defended and judged in Act III). There are also rules which govern the last scene (justice, pronouncement of judgement, the highest figure in authority speaks the final words) but the plays seem open structures or mirrors, organised around some themes, information about characters, loosely related actions, simple psychology, and recurrences.

The difficulty L. C. Knights and others have in locating significance in Shakespeare's narrative rather than in verse and imagery is perhaps explained by Beckerman's analysis of what he terms the dramaturgy, especially the various structural patterns and climaxes in the dramatic narrative. As the plays are episodic and not linked by causation, the action is not linear. Incidents do not follow each other in a succession of closely linked events. Shakespeare likes to alternate scenes to break up continuity. The climax is usually diffuse, a plateau rather than a compressed, intense scene. Because of the episodic nature of the plays and the way character, plot and rhetoric are of equal significance, there is no easily definable theme. Rather there are a number of mirrors which reflect upon each other. While Beckerman does not discuss the mirrors in *Coriolanus* there are obviously parallels between the relations of Coriolanus, Menenius and Volumnia to the community; the various ways Coriolanus, Aufidius, and Volumnia keep or fail to keep warrior notion of private honour; Volumnia's final triumph and Coriolanus' death; the plots of the tribunes and Aufidius' plot against Coriolanus. A Shakespeare play does not say, it offers a series of juxtapositions and contrasts which illuminate each other.

## Staging and some conventions

Consider *Coriolanus* from the standpoint of production, as does Styan (1967). The platform stage created intimacy and depth. It was wide and deep, with lots of space, many playing areas. Space was both localised and symbolic rather than realistic. There were two symmetrically arranged doors. Coriolanus [I.ix] is at one gate of Corioli; Cominius retreats at the other. The doors are used to show Coriolanus' valour in contrast to the others. He occupies a different space, has his own focus. The balcony provides other spaces, other places such as the walls of Corioli. Yet space is not distinct. It can be fluid and not realistically observed, more like a child's arbitrary world than the reality we know. Act v.vi of *Coriolanus* seems to be both in Antium and in Corioli, simultaneously; Shakespeare does not here distinguish between them but shifts the references back and forth as desired for the effect. The stage is symbolic rather than realistic. The Romans and Volsces are distinguished by their different costumes as opposing clans; but the costumes are not necessarily historically accurate. The main consideration is to distinguish people or groups visually and to provide a quick symbolical content. Coriolanus the soldier may be bloodied but he is also in a superior military costume. When he stands before the plebs in the gown of humility to ask their vote, we are aware of the gown as a humiliation, a symbol of a proud man being humiliated and ill at ease. Gestures are symbolic and convey a stronger meaning than on our stage. In *Coriolanus*, kneeling, the symbol of obedience, respect and supplication is used forcefully. Cominius, Coriolanus' former general, is reported to have kneeled to beg that Coriolanus not destroy Rome [v.i]. Volumnia again reverses roles by kneeling to her son; then Coriolanus' son kneels to him; finally all four – mother, wife, son and Valeria (symbol of Roman purity) – kneel. The effect is striking, ceremonial and unnatural in that the women and his son represent what Coriolanus most respects about the Roman code he claimed earlier to represent. Here are his bonds to Rome in supplication, unnaturally humiliating themselves (in contrast to his unwillingness to humiliate himself before the plebs).

Another symbolic, visual gesture is when Aufidius stands on the murdered Coriolanus in triumph and disrespect. Visually – gown of humility, women kneeling, Aufidius standing on Coriolanus – the play communicates a concern with domination, humiliation, status, power. Sometimes Shakespeare's stage directions are explicit. We see the 'mutinous citizens' with their 'weapons', then Coriolanus enters, war with the Volsces is announced and in a stage direction which upset Brecht and continues to upset many modern readers we are told 'Citizens steal away'.

In discussing conventions of grouping on the open stage Styan mentions that while Coriolanus is not addicted to soliloquies – he is not introspective like Hamlet – he is isolated from those on stage. He fights alone before the gates of Corioli, stands alone in the gown of humility, appears disguised at Aufidius' banqueting hall, faces his family by himself (with Aufidius looking on) and is dressed like a Roman when among the Volsces. If this heightens the individualism, it shows his alienation, loneliness, and suggests a potential rebel and traitor. He is part of no community.

Another convention is the use of oblique commentary; almost everyone in *Coriolanus* offers an opinion on the hero. There is continuous commentary on him from different perspectives. We do not see him from inside, which would privilege his point of view; we see him in public while others discuss his private emotions (ambition, attachment to mother, pride, etc.). Instead of the hero offering soliloquies to us, the tribunes several times finish a scene alone commenting on him. His character is seen in the round, he is inspected from different points of view and in relation to varied interests. These voices add to the richness of his character, the ambiguity and complexity, the fullness of the part. In keeping with the juxtapositional mode of the epic style, Shakespeare makes effective use of silence. Virgilia, by not speaking, offers a contrast to Volumnia, perhaps disapproving of her notions of dying for fame, perhaps simply showing how Coriolanus has failed to mature beyond his mother's influence into an independent man. Many statements in the play gain their strength by extreme understatement, suggesting irony or further depths. When Aufidius briefly says 'I was moved withal' in reply to Coriolanus' 'would you have heard a mother less?' we feel more is meant than said. Juxtapositions, silence, visual symbols and excessive information do not fit into a single interpretation. Critics too often give a one-dimensional reading, ignoring the richness that the play offers.

## The crowd

The ways in which Shakespeare communicates can be seen, as Styan says, by the treatment of the crowd. It is rarely just a mob. The play begins with the mutinous citizens (a reversal of what we would expect and an inversion of Renaissance notions of stage decorum). They speak first and gain equality, becoming in our mind a symbol of the community. Moreover they are individualised, though nameless, and have different points of view. The first citizen is radical, the second more conservative and understanding of the problems of the patricians and Coriolanus; the citizens are not on a rampage and need to discuss what they are doing and why. They even listen respectfully to Menenius. By contrast it may be felt that Coriolanus acts riotously when he first appears and begins insulting them. He may subdue them with contempt, they may feel defeated by the new situation created by Volscian attack but they are not contemptible early in the play. In Act II.iii 'Enter seven or eight citizens'. This is not a mob but different people who discuss a situation and have different points of view. They are courteous. They put up with Coriolanus' insolence and mockery. They discuss the situation and then, egged on by the tribunes who do seem contemptible, they become 'a rabble of plebeians with the Aediles' [III.i]. A reading of the play needs to give attention to such distinctions and changes in group psychology.

## Seven scenes of warfare: Act I.iv–x

Between I.iv and I.x, Shakespeare gives us seven scenes of warfare. Why not one? As the Romans are being beaten back, Coriolanus 'enters' separately cursing the retreating: he leads; the Volsces flee; 'he enters the gates' while the others fall back in fear. After we are told that he is dead, Coriolanus re-enters the stage, 'bleeding', 'assaulted by the enemy'. He is superior, clearly the hero in this world of battle in contrast to Coriolanus the ranting, dislikeable, proud patrician of scenes in Rome. But he is also foolhardy, great but likely to end badly. He takes too many risks. Next [I.v] 'enter certain Romans with their spoils'. The citizens' view of war! Here we are now on Coriolanus' side. He is bleeding and they are scavengers. Then [I.vi] 'enter Cominius, as it were in retire, with soldiers'. Is Cominius the voice of temperance or another one of Shakespeare's moderates who says the right thing in a way that convinces us that moderation is wrong? 'We are come

off / like Romans, neither foolish in our stands / Nor cowardly
in retire' [I.vi–xiii]. He might be right; but I want to be on
Coriolanus' side in any battle. As Cominius pontificates,
Coriolanus enters covered with blood 'come I too late?'
Hearing that Aufidius is near, Coriolanus wants to lead
volunteers against him. Again he is contrasted favourably
with 'the common file' and with Cominius, his supposed
superior. Coriolanus is a charismatic hero. The soldiers 'all
shout and wave their swords'. They take him up in their arms
and cast up their caps. In I.viii Aufidius and Martius engage
in a great slanging match. At the heart of such greatness is
the self not the state. The fight between states, clans, tribes,
classes, is about possessions, security, comfort, property.
Coriolanus is engaged in a personal combat over nobility and
dominance. This is a personal test. Here is the romantic
individual. The duel, one on one between the leaders, is ruined
when Volsces come in to the aid of Aufidius who is 'shamed'
by such help. This is the zenith of the play for both men.
Aufidius, beaten over and over by Coriolanus will in future
try to win by 'shame' and policy; he will become a mean-
spirited but eventually victorious realist, like the tribunes.
Coriolanus will soon be returned to the world of politicians,
words, hypocrisy in which he destroys himself through the
very virtues that make him a great hero.

These scenes, including I.x, are not just about fighting.
They are as rich in meaning as the political scenes. In earlier
societies these scenes would dominate the work of art; but
times have changed and politics now dominate the world of
the warrior. War does not really end, but peace is war in
masquerade, and Coriolanus is not good at such masquerades.
He is a dinosaur from an earlier era and cannot adjust. Or is
he? In *Coriolanus*, *Othello* and *Antony and Cleopatra*, Shakespeare
is interested in the vulnerability of the honest warrior in the
corrupt world of politics, social persuasion and words. But
why should this come up in Shakespeare's work at this time?
What is its context? And might it have some parallel to the
conflict between revenge and Christian mercy in the other
plays of this period? Does *Coriolanus* represent a chivalric
heroic world idealised in court literature, an Orlando Furioso,
an Almanzor, during a time when party, legal training, and

cunning will be more valuable than bravery and physical strength? Might he represent a feudal order remembered with nostalgia?

## Distancing

There are few soliloquies in *Coriolanus*. Its effect depends on action and the character in the community, a character with little observable inner life. The interplay between characters has its own complexity as when Aufidius observes Volumnia's pleading with Coriolanus. He brings into the scene other kinds of loyalties, values, dangers, perspectives than that between mother and son, Roman and Roman. It is such juxtapositions, contrasts, multiple perspectives which are the basis of Shakespeare's theatre and which make it epic. The focus shifts from class war to safety of state to personal honour to family to conflict between honouring a warrior and keeping him from political power by banishing him. The tribunes are mean-spirited, calculating, ignoble, ambitious, but they are correct in their assessment of Coriolanus and what he will do and they have as much justice on their side as he does. Aufidius studies him and ultimately wins. Knott and Burke show a hero trapped in the corridors of history, in a dead end; Paster suggests that rather than being a dead end, Coriolanus is the great individual the community needs for its survival. Such complexity and such objectivity need the distance and fragmentary scenes that we find in the epic theatre. It is what Brecht wanted but was seldom able to achieve as he also wanted to control the meaning or created too much empathy for characters.

## An historical style: the house of mirrors

Seeing the literature of the past through the eyes of postmodernist literature and recent critical theory, most criticism appears to be a fiction, fictions which seldom seem solidly grounded in much textual evidence. The older critics may have misread or interpreted with naïve assumptions about the unity of the text but the textual evidence was in itself of interest. Increasingly interpretations, contexts, theories seem words, words, words. How to get out of the labyrinth in which one fiction leads to another? Beckerman's analysis of Shakespeare's plays at the Globe Theatre offers a way out. It may be scholarly fiction but the analysis is testable. The notion of an Elizabethan or Jacobean play as a house of mirrors with no clearly articulated central theme and the idea of the equality of the plot, character and imagery corresponds to my experience of *Coriolanus*. It is not a new idea. It is generally accepted that the late Renaissance thought by analogies and constructed works of art with double plots, reflectors, multiple symbols and perspectives. There is a recognisable historical style by which to read *Coriolanus* which corresponds to our notion of openness, decentredness, and post-modernism. It is not a matter of Beckerman being right or wrong. He offers a way to discuss *Coriolanus* which still corresponds to the text and to ways of studying Renaissance art and literature that have in the past proved valuable.

In the house of mirrors called *Coriolanus* certain themes, image patterns, concerns, and kinds of psychology seem foregrounded and predominant, calling attention to them selves, demanding awareness, requiring recognition regardless of how they are interpreted. There are such themes as virtue and pride, self-hood versus community, language and persuasion, planning and deceit, role-playing and directing others, the influence of sexual attraction and of emotional dependency on individual and communal conduct, the necessity and futility of politics (and perhaps all relations). The way Shakespeare builds by juxtapositions, the excess of information provided about characters, the gaps in characterisation and narration, the way a Shakespearean text aims at a multiplicity of significances, the richness of imagery, means that themes multiply from the evidence of the text.

## The isolated hero's tragedy

*Coriolanus* is one of the plays of the tragic period which while showing the hypocrisies and corruptions of the society, reveal the impossibility of living outside social groups. The individual's relationship to society is also explored in *Othello* where the Moor as an outsider to Venice and civilian society is easily misled by Iago. Coriolanus' sense of superiority as warrior and noble, his hatred of the hypocritical politicians and the conniving isolates him from society, makes him a victim of those who are cunning and clever in manipulating others. While many of Shakespeare's plays give us a sense of a Christian spiritual order transcending society, some plays of the tragic period – especially those with classical pagan settings – offer no feelings of spiritual consolation contrasting to the dog-eat-dog savageness of secular life. In these plays the hero is isolated but without hope of moral and spiritual redemption.

Coriolanus is a classic hero of the epic, superhumanly brave, alone, true to himself and his warrior sense of virtue; but his bravery and truth to his code is tragic: it leads him to insult others for their lack of bravery and he appears proud to those who expect leaders to court and flatter them. As a result he damns his own chances to become a leader in his society; such leadership is expected from someone of his achievement and family.

There is no place Coriolanus can live; he is too proud of his achievements as a soldier and noble (in his eyes the two are related; to be a warrior is to embody the ideal of his class) to accept the humiliation required of him in Rome as a necessary part of the political process. Among the Volsces he is easy prey to the manipulations of others and when challenged reverts to the anger and pride which ruined him in Rome and which is even less acceptable among his former enemies to whom he has now broken a pledge. There is no final triumph, reconciliation, confession, forgiveness or self-knowledge at the end of *Coriolanus*. The ending is not even ambiguous; it is perhaps demoralised, 'Let's make the best of it' [v.vi.147].

## The hero, society and honour

There is a long literary tradition of the warrior hero who in being true to his own valour and honour spurns the softness, luxury, corruption and hypocrisy of society; he fights for himself not for a master or a state. Eventually, however, he falls in love and is conquered by a woman. As he woos the woman and transfers his personal sense of honour to fighting for her honour, he begins the process of socialisation; his freedom and energy are put at her disposal and then are harnessed to the state through his marriage to her. His male freedom and aggression become channelled through her into socially useful actions; love and marriage redirect his libido, making him part of a community whereas previously he was at war with everyone.

Coriolanus is similar to such a classical hero in his seeming invulnerability, anger, pride, ready tongue, sense of self-hood and belief in the virtue of his warrior code with his proud notion of honour, valour, and so on. War for him is a time when the individual can shine and be true to himself. War and battle destroy the hypocrisies of peaceful society and enable one to be superior over others. The warrior fights for himself and his honour, not for the city and wealth. But this is what irritates the tribunes about Coriolanus. They want a soldier under their command, they want soldiers who claim their fight is for the people and the state. They want a servant who will obey them and those they represent, they want to be top dog; but for Coriolanus war is competition for martial valour and honour, not a fight between two communities for wealth, resources, property. The epitome of Coriolanus' epic code is the man-to-man, hand-to-hand, fight between two great soldiers to prove which is number one, who is the best.

Coriolanus' code goes back before the modern state to a time of independent warriors, who fought for themselves. Coriolanus has been educated to such a code by his mother, who like other members of the nobility holds ideals about a warrior's value; but, in fact, as in shown by the play, his mother sees such virtue as at the service of the state. The difference between mother's and son's view of valour is partly ideological, partly psychological. For the mother there is no conflict between state and self because the state and Roman nobility are one. No contradiction exists for her between fighting for self-honour, fighting for Rome and performing duties as a noble; they are the same. Faced by signs of conflict her instinct is to keep the community together through compromise and hypocrisy. For her there is no difference between war and peace; politics are a kind of war in which words are used instead of arms. She tells her son to win by speech over the commoners what he wants to win by force of arms. Since honour for her means honour by the state, to destroy Rome is to destroy one's name. She will die in suicide rather than share such dishonour. Honour can only come from Rome, it is given by a society of which she sees herself as part despite evidence that the society is severely divided into classes and that a change is taking place which will weaken the dominance of the class to which she belongs and with which she identifies Rome. It is arguable that the values she has taught her son are a confusing mixture of warrior, class and patriotic duties which made sense until they were challenged by the claims of another class to govern and share in the economy. As a mother she fulfilled her duty to her class by teaching her son to be a fearless warrior for Rome; she continues to fulfil her duty and its ideal of dominance through service to the state when she persuades her son not to destroy Rome.

For Coriolanus the situation is different and indeed it has changed. Emotionally Coriolanus is not part of a larger community; he feels himself part of a class which he believes has made Rome. He sees himself born to rule by exemplifying the values of his class, especially those of a warrior. But the more he lives up to the values taught by his mother, the more he will be alienated from others, since others are not the fearless superhero at which he aims. His most brave and characteristic actions are bound to give rise to envy, animosity, and lead to his alienation and isolation by exceeding the behaviour of others. Even the enemy warrior Aufidius, whose hatred of Coriolanus appears a perverted love, so envies him that he resorts to treachery and lies to destroy him.

But as important as Coriolanus' god-like excess of virtue and his overly literal belief in his mother's ideal there is the changed political situation. The lower classes now have a say in government through their representatives and it is clear from the play that this amounts to a controlling interest since the tribunes as voice of the people have veto power. They gain free grain and prevent Coriolanus from consularship in both tests by threatening civil war. As Rome and the nobility are no longer one, there is a contradiction which Coriolanus understands but which the patricians refuse to face and attempt to avoid facing through appeasement and compromise, acts which shift power to the tribunes. The rights of the commoners to deny consularship is an ancient if seldom used right. What is new is the right to elect tribunes. The tribunes create an organised political focus around discontents, economic drives and fears, turning the populace into a class with a consciousness of itself, its demands and its own potential power.

Coriolanus claims for himself the values of the past, especially an older (feudal) code of personal and family honour – nobility expressed in action by soldiership and in conduct by contempt of those who are not nobles or of gentle birth. Coriolanus' code of the warrior's superiority through his prowess has been challenged by the tribunes and commoners – those who claim rights without fighting for them in the field of battle against external enemies. He is like a chivalric warrior who, faced by modern notions of democracy, retreats into a feudal or ancient code of personal glory. If for him the people are the Other, not Rome, the tribunes see him in similar terms as an enemy, who will take away both their new positions in the government and the people's ancient rights. For them Rome consists of the people, a term which seems only to include the commoners they represent but not the nobility. What particularly irritates them about Coriolanus and makes them hate his virtues is that his victories are for himself, his mother and his upper-class vision of Rome. By showing that Rome requires his nobility, his valiantness, Coriolanus implies that the commons, the non-soldiers, are disqualified from rights to dignity and political power.

Coriolanus begins as a Roman and symbolically becomes a child. As the Roman ideal is challenged by class, it shatters and Coriolanus is driven outside society fighting for his own notion of honour and revenge. This is undermined by the effect of his mother on him. A curious situation then develops at the play's conclusion in which Coriolanus is both reduced to the boy who once learned his ideals from his mother and is returned to society to be killed.

*Coriolanus*, rather than showing how the hero with his masculine values becomes part of society, shows how such values and energy make the hero different, isolated from society. This is the story of the warrior after marriage, of someone who cannot integrate and accommodate, and who in his own view would be humiliated by coming to an arrangement with the existing social situation. He is, however, through his mother temporarily persuaded to attempt to accommodate himself to civil society. Significantly, it is through the love of his mother, rather than a female friend, mistress or wife, that he is persuaded to go before the people to plead for his consularship, and his love for his mother causes him to return again to the people to try to win them; his mother persuades him not to take his revenge on Rome. The result in each case is a disaster, the last of which results in his death. It could be said that Shakespeare shows the impossibility of realisation of the warrior ideals in the political–social world. Surrounded by mother, wife, less heroic nobles, political class pressures, jealousies, the heroic ideal turns out to be disastrous; viewed with a little psychology, the hero is found to be a mother's boy destroyed by momma's ambition to be a respected leader of society.

## Shakespeare's recurrent themes and techniques

Most authors have their 'bag' of themes, scenes, characters, obsessions, mannerisms, ideas, structures, which recur throughout their work and which develop, evolve and change in significant ways. *Coriolanus* offers a new treatment of a number of Shakespeare's recurring themes such as the causes of evil, the divorce between language and reality, the destructive manipulation of the naïve by those who can shape social action, the role of hypocrisy in life, the futility yet necessity of political and social action, the dominating role of some women, the alienation of the hero, the self-destructiveness of anger, and so on. The play also is a further development in the ironic distancing inherent to epic theatre, reveals a contrasting development in the use of affective scenes and the linking of domestic and personal with the public. There is a greater

individualisation of language and style reflected in new liberties with the iambic pentameter and syntax. There is a further
questioning, even a deconstruction of the tragic. Perhaps most
significant, acting, directing, writing scripts for others, is
treated here as both normal to society and evil. The theatre
and language seem to bring destruction.

There are other themes of interest. Coriolanus' relationship
with his mother follows Hamlet's intensity of feeling for his
mother. (And this is another play with a missing or displaced
father.) Like *Hamlet* this is a play where the state becomes a
corrupt prison from which the hero is only liberated by exile,
while his attempt to return and find revenge ends in his death.
Coriolanus' unjust trial by the citizens in Rome and his trial
at the end of the play recalls the many trial scenes in
Shakespeare's plays ranging from Hamlet's attempt to try
Claudius (the play within the play and the prayer scene) to
the more relevant scenes in *Measure for Measure* where a corrupt
Angelo controls the power of justice and Isabella is helpless,
the scenes in *King Lear* where the king tries his daughters, and
Gloucester's trial. The total impression is that there is no
justice in this world in Shakespeare's plays (and perhaps it
can only be found in Christian mercy). *Coriolanus* is in some
ways the most horrifying example of justice perverted because
the hero is stripped and declared a traitor not by hypocrites
but by the mass of the people led by demagogues. Coriolanus
contributes to his own downfall, but after seeing this play who
would ever trust a trial by one's peers again?

Usually there is some pretence at the end of Shakespeare's
plays that suffering has been worthwhile. Cleopatra symbolically triumphs by cheating Ceasar of his triumph, by her
death which is viewed as marriage to Antony. Hamlet revenges
his father; Fortinbras will rule and set right what appears to
have been an injustice caused by Hamlet's father. We may
feel that Angelo has not reformed and that Isabella is being
pushed into marriage which she may not want, but the three
marriages at the end of *Measure for Measure* formally conclude
the play with a feeling of renewal and justice satisfied.
*Coriolanus* offers no symbolic satisfactions. Coriolanus' life has
been wasted for what? Nothing has changed. Rome is neither
more unified nor safe. Coriolanus' mother is now a hero but

few will feel that the mother's success is admirable. Signs of futility have always been there in the plays and increasingly so in the tragic period but *Coriolanus* appears to be a play which accepts that life has no purpose outside what might be gained in a futile world of corruption, hypocrisy and evil ambition.

*Coriolanus* shares with many of Shakespeare's plays the theme of wrath (anger or choler). The hero or main character in a moment of mad anger brings down his world, ruins what he has or destroys what he loves. Othello in jealousy killing Desdemona is one version of the theme; King Lear first in anger disinherits Cordelia, then in anger destroys what nest he has left with his two daughters. Coriolanus is a prisoner of wrath, 'wrath overwhelmed my pity' [I.ix.84]. The tribunes know that it is easy putting him into a rage; it is possible to take advantage of his choler to prevent his election. They wait for him 'to fall in rage' and 'anger'. And that is just what happens in III.i and III.iii. So there is no doubt that the audience of *Coriolanus* or the citizens understand what is happening, several speeches prepare us for Coriolanus' self-destructive anger. Menenius warns him to be calm; there is the rather funny exchange:

> MENENIUS.  His choler?
> CORIOLANUS.  Choler!
> Were I as patient as the midnight sleep,
> By Jove, 'twould be my mind.
> [III.i.82–5]

Menenius warns him 'Put not your worthy rage into your tongue' [III.i.239]. His mother says that he should have a brain as well as a heart and learn like her the 'use of anger' [III.ii.30]. And III.ii concludes with Cominius, Menenius and Coriolanus all supposedly agreed that he must speak 'mildly' to the citizens at his trial. Having twice ruined himself in Rome by displays of anger, he once again falls into the trap in Corioli, giving Aufidius an excuse to kill him. One of the great ironies of the play is that cunning Aufidius not only works Coriolanus into a rage but then pretends rage to kill him. Nothing can be more cynical than Aufidius' 'My rage is gone, / And I am struck with sorrow' [v.vi.147–8]. This is partly a play about the destructive effects of anger.

## Language and acting as deception

Since the popularity of post-modern fiction and critical theories which see a text as a construction, it has become commonplace to say that literature can either imitate reality or be concerned with the art of art and that it more likely, or more interestingly, is concerned with the latter. Shakespeare's plays always have a concern with the nature of language, spectacle, playing and directing, treating each as a danger, an untruth, a potential source of evil. Perhaps he had a writer's distrust for words? The villains of his plays – Richard III, Iago, Edmund – are the wordsmiths, the ones who make up the plots, who arrange scenes that deceive. The best speakers, the playwrights, are evil. If they are not (Prospero is a major exception) they are aware of the potential of art to do evil. *Coriolanus* is filled with playlets, rehearsals, roles, acting. It is also a play where Shakespeare does not fall back on a possible devil theory of evil. Richard III and Iago are in part traditional vice characters. Iago gives many explanations for his conduct but he is finally someone whose malcontentedness seems devilish rather than of human origins. In the case of the tribunes, the nobles, Aufidius, there are no devils; they are driven by recognisable human ambitions, the desire for power, fear, envy. The self-referentiality of the play is not therefore an abstract theoretical concern with the art of drama; rather the play questions whether language, the ability to deceive others, the art of falsifying may in itself be a moral danger, not only untrue but evil in origin because false and most likely used to deceive the innocent. Consider that opening scene in *King Lear*. Language is used to lie, truth cannot flatter. Coriolanus' best quality is that he cannot lie. What he says may be dislikeable, hateful, but it is not flattery, does not cover secret aims.

## Revelations of character

Characters appear to change during the course of the play –
as in Coriolanus' case because of circumstances – or because
we are given more information and see in new ways. Characters are either unstable or unlikeable. Aufidius is perhaps
too much of a function to be regarded as evidence but there
is the obvious case of Menenius. At first we are told that he
is 'honest' and 'one that has always loved the people'. But the
people do not seem to realise that his speech to them about
the state as a body and his blaming the drought on the gods
is patrician ideology and propaganda. Part of his effectiveness
is the bubbling, old honesty he pretends. He tells the tribunes
'what I think, I utter, and spend my malice in my breath'
[II.i.55]. Later, however, whatever he says is likely to be a lie
or premeditated for political effect. He is like the tribunes,
Aufidius and Volumnia, in trying to use Coriolanus for his
own ends. Like many moderate figures he is made a bit absurd
by Shakespeare. He is convinced that the world consists of
people like himself who are governed by simple comforts and
desires, and that all he needs do is to appeal to Coriolanus
after the latter has eaten and is 'dieted to my request'. It is
difficult not to see either Menenius' predatory nature or
Shakespeare's ironic attitude towards him in the language
'then I'll set upon him' [v.i.58]. Before the Volsces, he speaks
of Coriolanus in such a way that detracts from the warrior's
achievement and makes us wonder if Menenius always lies.
He claims he has always amplified and 'varnished' Coriolanus.
He appears absurd when he asks 'has he dined?' Where is
the spontaneous, honest tongue he claimed? The speech to
Coriolanus is such an awkward clumsy artificial mess that it
seems likely Shakespeare has the knife into Menenius and is
making certain that we judge him. It will be noticed that most
of the characters except Coriolanus are made less attractive
after Act III.

## Coriolanus and his mother

At the core of each of Shakespeare's plays is some fundamental

human problem, a failed rite of passage such as the unwillingness of a father to give up his daughter's love (*King Lear*) or
the way jealousy turns into destructive rage (*Othello, Winter's
Tale*). Hamlet although 30 years old seems immature in his
idealisation of his father and his emotional attachment to his
mother.

Early in the play the First Citizen says the services Coriolanus has done are not for his country but 'to please his mother'
[i.i.39]. His mother speaks of him both as a husband and as
someone she would sacrifice for the fame it brought: 'If my
son were my husband I should freelier rejoice in that absence
wherein he won honour, than in the embracements of his bed
where he would show most love' [i.iii.2–6]. Coriolanus says
his mother 'has a charter to extol her blood' but this 'grieves
me' [i.iv.16–18]. Her praise and his embarrassment seem
revealing of an adolescent's relationship to a parent from
whom he has not become emotionally independent. Volumnia
calls him 'my boy' [ii.i.105], 'my son' [142], 'my good soldier'
[ii.i.105] and when they first are together in the play she needs
remind him of 'thy wife' [ii.i.183] to whom Coriolanus says
only 'O my sweet lady, pardon' [ii.i.188].

Coriolanus is dominated by his mother who persuades him
to seek the consularship she wants for him. 'Why force you
this?' [iii.ii.51]. She replies 'I am in this your wife' [iii.ii.65],
'My son, go to them' [iii.ii.72–3], 'Go and be ruled' [iii.ii.90].
He becomes her performing dog: 'My praises made thee first
a soldier, so,/To have my praise for this, perform a part'
[iii.ii.108–9]. Volumnia can win any argument by rejecting
him: 'Thy valiantness was mine, thou suck'st it from me,/But
owe that pride thyself'. To which he replies 'Mother, I am
going to the market place:/Chide no more' [iii.iii.129–30,
131–2]. A leader of the army, a man-killer who single handed
conquers a city and he pleads 'Chide no more'! When
Coriolanus loses his temper before the crowd Menenius says
'Is this the promise that you made your mother?' [iii.iii.85].
Later, after he is banished from Rome and taking farewell
from his mother he tells her to cheer up and implicitly
compares himself both to Hercules and to a husband:

Resume that spirit you were wont to say,

> If you had been the wife of Hercules,
> Six of his labours you'd have done, and saved
> Your husband so much sweat.
>
> [IV.i.16–18]

Later Volumnia recommends to Virgilia that she imitates her in lamenting 'in anger, Juno like' [IV.ii.53]. Juno is both goddess of Rome and the wife of Jupiter.

Coriolanus seeking revenge on Rome claims 'wife, mother, child, I know not' [v.ii.74], but as soon as he sees his mother, wife and his child he fears he will be 'tempted to infringe' his 'vow / In the same time 'tis made' [v.iii.21]. His mother bows and he is disturbed, feeling a reversal of the universal order, 'As if Olympus to a molehill should / In supplication nod' [30–1]. He is so stirred that he must attempt to harden himself in his will (a sign, of course, that he is likely to reverse himself):

> . . . I'll never
> Be such a gosling to obey instinct, but stand
> As if a man were author of himself
> And knew no other kin.
>
> [v.iii.34–7]

Despite his assertions that he is an individual with a strong sense of himself, Coriolanus has strong ties to his family, especially to his mother, which undermine his claim to selfhood. His mother is the focus of his feelings. She persuaded him to stand for consul, to stand trial by the people and now she persuades him to give up his revenge. Rather than the great hero who said he will banish Rome by going into exile, he is found to be a tearful boy unable to resist his mother's scolding. He cannot even follow his own self-interest. She is 'the most noble mother in the world' [v.iii.49] to whom he kneels in homage. She needs only to kneel in supplication before him for him to be disturbed and find the situation unnatural, although as a powerful conqueror he is to be supplicated. That he is disturbed by the symbolism shows that under the god-like public aspect remains an immature child. Except for minor interjections from the other characters

the remainder of v.iii takes place between Volumnia and
Coriolanus. Their relationship is one play, a drama between
a dominant mother and a rebellious but dominated son. Her
principles have made him what he is; he lives by her words.
She will destroy him now rather than let him ruin her vision
of herself as a superior patrician mother who sacrifices her
sons for Rome. Having no other son to sacrifice to the country,
she can only sacrifice him. Nobility is birth, manner, conduct,
position. She increases her nobility (fame in Rome) by
destroying his nobility (valiantness as soldier; truth to his
integrity of self and class).

Cominius and Menenius could not persuade Coriolanus to
listen to their pleas; but Volumnia plays on him as son, lover,
ungrateful son; 'Thou art my warrior / I holp frame thee'
[v.iii.62–3]. Coriolanus hardly has a chance and is already
weakening: [v.vi.78–86] 'I beseech you . . . tell me not . . .
desire me not / T'allay my rages and revenges with / Your
colder reasons'. Volumnia's speech [v.iii.94–125] with its 'we'
merges Coriolanus' wife and child with herself in a more
sophisticated appeal than Menenius' awkward, trite claim
upon his relationship ('O my son, my son') [v.ii.73]. Where
Menenius cries and supplicates, Volumnia, having first estab-
lished an emotional bond between the family and Coriolanus,
now indicates that her loyalties to Rome are as great as, even
greater, than her love for her son. The situation is tricky since
outright rejection of Coriolanus could lead to one of his rages;
she leads him on, slowly breaking down his resolve to be
independent. Then when his family emotions have returned,
she starts turning away from him until he gives in. She involves
him in her dilemma, rather than showing interest in his hurts,
so that she can threaten him. She fudges and blurs boundaries
between Rome and family ('whereto we were bound . . . the
country, our dear nurse'). As she does this it first appears that
she will not choose between son and country (or . . . or, either
. . . or else) and that whether he is victor or loser he is a
humiliation in her eyes. He will either 'be led with manackles
through our streets' as a loser (which we know is unlikely) or
if he wins he will be celebrated for 'having bravely shed / Thy
wife and children's blood'. Having portrayed victory over
Rome as equivalent to bloody murder of his family she further

works on his emotions by threatening suicide. She begins this part of the persuasion with 'son' and with reference to herself. 'For myself, son / I propose not to wait.' After the mocking of him in 'bravely' ('bravely shed / Thy wife and children's blood') the use of such phrases as 'For myself', 'I', 'son', personalises the situation, making Coriolanus' revenge not on Rome but on his family and especially on her:

> . . . thou shalt no sooner
> March to assault thy country than to tread
> . . . on thy mother's womb
> That brought thee to this world.

The image of 'tread' which occurs in key moments of the play shifts here from 'tread on the country's ruin' [v.iii.116] to 'tread . . . on thy mother's womb'.

His son's 'A shall not tread on me' [127] provides another mirror, supporting the notion that war on Rome is war on his family; he cannot take revenge on one without warring with the other.

## Persuasion and dependency

As in the history plays civil war becomes war between members of a family. This does not imply that Shakespeare believes what Volumnia argues. He is dramatising someone persuading another person, and we are made conscious of this as a scene of persuasion. It is preceded by two similar attempts to change Coriolanus' mind and by parallels to Menenius' speech. Moreover we recall earlier scenes in which Volumnia worked on his emotions, turning him into a dependent child. And we are aware of her willingness, even eagerness to sacrifice him, for her reputation in Rome: 'his good report should have been my son; I therein would have found issue . . . had I a dozen sons . . . I had rather had eleven die for the country' [I.iii.21–6].

The second part of Volumnia's speech [v.iii.131–82] uses many of the same tricks, complaining and scolding, that she had used in Rome when persuading Coriolanus:

> . . . There's no man in the world
> More bound to's mother, yet here he lets me prate
> Like one i'th sticks. Thou hast never in thy life
> Showed thy dear mother any courtesy,
> When she, poor hen, fond of no second brood,
> Has clucked thee to the wars, and safely home
> Loaded with honour.

As the scene continues the three women and the son kneel in a striking image of supplication. But Volumnia's words are not those of a supplicant. As often in the play the visual and the aural offer contrasting messages. She both reminds him of family ties and rejects him:

> So, we will home to Rome
> And die among our neighbours. . . .
> This fellow had a Volscian to his mother;
> His wife is in Corioles, and his child
> Like him by chance.
>
> [v.iii.122–5]

Faced by rejection, curses, sentiment, motherly appeals, Coriolanus is conquered and after a long dramatic silence typical of his truth to his inner self, he breaks down in tears and cries 'O, mother, mother: / What have you done?' [v.iii.182–3]. He knows this will lead to his death, 'Most dangerously you have with him prevailed'. She says nothing. It is typical of Shakespeare's technique that there should be this silence where we might expect the mother and Virgilia to respond or show some concern about the danger they have brought on Coriolanus, some celebration of their victory, or an attempt to persuade him to go back to Rome with them. We can make up fictions, assume it is Coriolanus' sense of honour which leads him back to Corioli rather than Rome but in fact we know nothing, the focus shifts away from the relationship between Coriolanus and Aufidius.

## Crying

Even more striking than the kneeling and the holding of
Volumnia by the hand is the information that Coriolanus is
crying: 'it is no little thing to make / Mine eyes to sweet
compassion' [v.iii.196]. This echoes the tears of Menenius in
v.ii.74 ('here's water') which may or may not be spontaneous.
It is characteristic of Shakespeare's objectivity that we do not
know if Volumnia is any more sincere than Menenius – she
indeed may be less – or just a better, more skilled pleader.
(When we learn that the citizens in v.iv are now attacking the
tribunes they formerly worshipped, we know what Shakespeare
probably thinks of their inconsistency. The Third Conspirator
tells Aufidius the people are only interested in results and
accept whoever is in power [v.vi.17–18].) But those tears are
extraordinary and will be recalled several times in the final
scene by Aufidius. They suggest Coriolanus' immaturity. Here
is a warrior who has killed men crying at his mother's claim
that he never does what she wants (which we know is false)
and that she will kill herself if he takes his revenge on Rome.
How does this differ from an immature, childish quarrel and
its threats? Shakespeare's magic is to ground themes of mercy
and honour in such psychology. Various parallels and mirrors
occur in v.iv when the tribune Sicinius says that Coriolanus
'loved his mother dearly'. 'There is no more mercy in him
than milk in a male tiger' [v.iv.29–30].

Masculinity is a theme of the play. The Roman notion of
maleness is of hard, unflinching, bloodiness. Volumnia claims
that blood 'becomes a man' [v.iii.42–3], in 'cruel war' Coriolanus 'had proved himself a man' [v.iii.19]. Significantly, when
he is beginning to crack under the emotional assault of
Volumnia, Virgilia and his son, Coriolanus says 'Not a
woman's tenderness to be / Requires nor child nor woman's
face to see' [v.iii.129–30]. The shift into rhyme is a convention
of Jacobean drama used for scenes of emotional heightening,
formality, symbolism, comments to the audience, another
departure from realism.

Volumnia enters Rome [v.v] in triumph, recalling Coriolanus' triumph in ii.i. This contrasts with v.vi where Coriolanus
attempts to enter Corioli (another parallel) in triumph and

will die for having betrayed the Volsces for 'a few drops of women's rheum' [v.vi.46]. 'For certain drops of salt' [93] 'At his nurse's tears / he whined' [97]. He is 'a boy of tears' [101]. It is the word 'boy' which Coriolanus cannot bear. This sets off his rage. If he entered Corioli knowing the situation was dangerous, he now explodes through all his caution and repeats his former self-destructive behaviour, bragging how he killed Volscians: 'Boy!! O Slave!' [60], 'Boy! False Hound!' [111], 'Alone I did it. Boy!' [116].

The hero lives in a world of lesser people with petty ambitions and ugly plots who gang up to exile and kill him. His mother for all her pride turns out to be like them.

## Sex, love and bonding

Coriolanus is not mature; he is emotionally still a boy. This implication is furthered by sexual imagery which is rather focused on the relationship between the soldier and other men than on him and women. Wilson Knight felt that Coriolanus as a killing machine was conquered by love, a force of good. I see love in the play as something demanded by society, by Coriolanus' mother and as an immature weakness of Coriolanus. Aufidius sticks to his desire for revenge and emerges victorious over his rival at the play's end.

Shakespeare early establishes the use of sexual imagery in treating the relationship between the two warriors. They are like lovers. When Coriolanus (who is still Martius) sees Cominius on the battlefield:

> O, let me clip ye
> In arms as sound as when I wooed; in heart
> As merry as our nuptial day was done,
> And tapers burned to bedward.
> [I.v.29–32]

Shakespeare will not treat the relationship between Coriolanus and his wife Virgilia with such sexual emotion, indeed she is so silent in the play as almost not to exist. In his relationship with Aufidius, Coriolanus uses the language of hate as if it were intense love: 'I'll fight with none but thee', 'We hate alike' [I.viii.11–13]. In their fight for dominance, they stimulate each other to excitement: 'Let the first budger die the other's slave, / And the gods doom him after!'

> Alone I fought in your Corioles walls,
> And made what work I pleased: tis not my blood
> Wherein thou seest me masked. For thy revenge,
> Wrench thou thy power to th'highest."
>
> [I.viii.8–11]

(This looks forward to 'Alone I did it' [v.vi.116].) Later, defeated by Coriolanus, Aufidius says 'If e'er again I meet him beard to beard, / He's mine, or I am his' [I.x.11–12]. He wants to 'Wash my fierce hand in's heart' [I.x.29]. Suggestion of the sexuality of battle is also seen in Cominius' description of Coriolanus 'When he might act the woman in the scene, / He proved best man i'th'field' [II.ii.98–9]. Within Roman values to be a victorious fighter is to be a man. A boy is a woman until he has proved himself as Coriolanus did although he still had an 'Amazonian chin' [II.ii.93].

## The virgin warrior: fear of contamination

Coriolanus objects to putting on the gown of humility, he says he cannot 'stand naked' and entreat the people [II.ii.139]. The imagery of sexual modesty is continued with 'It is a part / That I shall blush in acting' [147–8]. Sexuality, besides being part of fights for dominance, is part of acting, playing roles, persuading others, especially in politics or in relationships. Coriolanus feels playing to the public is prostitution of his truth to himself; it spoils his integrity. To entreat others is to buy votes. It also transfers power to them. Your value is no longer what you do; it is what others say you are. The themes of power, domination and origins of value keep being expressed in images of food, money and sex. How you love and are loved is how you are nourished, paid, valued and nourish, pay, value. Coriolanus believes his right to be consul by his 'own desert' [II.iii.68]. He has made himself on the battlefield. He lives by an image of himself. To stand before the people means he is for 'hire' [II.ii.152]. The citizens also see their power as sexual: 'We are to put our tongues into these wounds' [III.i.6]. Images of tongues link speaking to the sexual and the many blood images in the play (blood as breeding, as self, as what makes him a man, and which the public wants revealed to it almost as looking at his private parts). When Coriolanus first appears in the gown of humility, he objects: 'I cannot bring my tongue to such a place' [II.ii.55]. His mockery of the citizens is in sexual terms. When they object 'you have not loved the common people', Coriolanus replies that he is 'the more virtuous that I have not been common in my love' [II.iii.98–9]. If common here links the love of the people and the commoners and prostitution, there is exhibited, as elsewhere in the play, a strong attraction–hate relationship in dependency. Coriolanus loves–hates his mother on whom he is dependent. Aufidius will come to hate Coriolanus on whom he becomes dependent as a warrior. The people want to be loved. Menenius tells the people 'most charitable care / Have the patricians of you' [I.i.67–8]. The First Citizen replies 'care for us? . . . They ne'er cared for us yet. Suffer us to famish' [I.i.81–2]. To love and care for is to protect, to nourish, be intimate with. The people are attracted to Coriolanus as a victor, but when he spurns them they want to kill him. His fear of contamination by the people is almost sexual; but he needs them if he is to be consul, so his own dependency on them may explain the intensity of his hatred.

## The price of love: unclean mouths

Coriolanus' unwillingness to reveal his wounds makes him seem an innocent guarding virginity. The terms he uses to describe the citizens refer to their lack of cleanliness, their bad breath. This may well have been a fact of the time; but Coriolanus seems as obsessed as if contact were sexual intimacy. When the citizens ask for his love, Coriolanus mocks 'I will counterfeit the bewitchment of some popular man and give a bountiful to the desirers' [II.iii.106–7]. He will only show his wounds in private [II.iii.80–1,172]. The wound, blood, sexual imagery becomes degraded into prostitution and is linked with the imagery of money, price, cost, reflecting the citizens' perspective but also associated with the futility of life. Exchanges are often treated as the buying of sexual favours:

> THIRD CITIZEN.    You must think, if we give you anything, we hope to gain by you.
> CORIOLANUS.    Well then, I pray, your price, o'th'consulship?
> FIRST CITIZEN.    The price is, to ask it kindly.
> CORIOLANUS.    Kindly, sir, I pray let me ha't. I have wounds to show you, which shall be yours in private.    [II.ii.73–81]

Throughout the play the relationship between Coriolanus and Aufidius is tinged with mutual admiration that borders on the sexual. Coriolanus asks whether Aufidius discusses him: 'Spoke he of me?' No teenager could be more eager: 'How? What?' 'He would pawn fortunes . . . so he might / Be called your vanquisher'. 'I wish I had a cause to seek him there' [III.i.12–19]. The ironic foreshadowing of how Coriolanus' wishes will be fulfilled should not distract from the contrast between Coriolanus' attraction towards Aufidius (which is mutual) and his hatred of 'The tongue o'th'common mouth' [III.i.22].

Coriolanus does not like speech and associates defilement with tongues, stinking breath, prostitution of honour through words and hypocrisy. His words are direct, like blows, honest, and often angry. He seems to view the tribunes especially in sexual terms as a contamination: 'sedition' has been 'ploughed for, sowed / by mingling them with us' [III.iii.70–1]. Since the 'tribunes are the people's mouth' [III.i.269], the mutual hatred of Coriolanus and the tribunes is to be expected. Coriolanus is not the first to feel that mixing of the classes, races, castes, clans, of self or identity with others is sexual defilement. His vocabulary mingles the sexual and physical with many other themes of the play such as the body politic and images of feeding: 'How shall this bosom multiplied digest? / The Senate's courtesy?' 'Thus we debase / the nature of our seats.' The rabble 'will in time / Break ope the locks o'th'Senate' [III.i.130–6]. Those who 'love the fundamental part of state' will want to 'pluck out / the multitudinous tongue, let them not lick / The sweet. . . . Your dishonour'. [III.i.150, 154, 156]. The associations between tongue, sexuality and masculinity are obvious. 'Put not your worthy rage into your tongue' [III.i.239]; 'His heart's his mouth / What his breast forges, his tongue must vent' [254–5]. Cominius who is always calculating and lacks daring sees this as 'manhood' turned into 'foolery' [266].

## Pretending love: inconstancy

Even Volumnia speaks of winning over the crowd in terms of pretending to be in love:

> Say to them
> Thou art their soldier, and being bred in broils
> Hast not the soft way which, thou dost confess,
> Were fit for thee to use, as they to claim,
> In asking their good love; but thou wilt frame
> Thyself, forsooth, hereafter theirs.
>
> [III.ii.80–5]

(This is what Coriolanus does at the play's conclusion when he returns to Corioli: 'I am returned your soldier, / No more infected with my country's love' [v.vi.71–2].) Coriolanus feels prostituted, humiliated, soiled.

> Must I go show them my unbarbed sconce? Must I
> With my base tongue give to my noble heart
> A lie that he must bear?
>
> [III.ii.99–101]

He feels 'possessed' with 'Some harlot's spirit', his 'throat of war' unmanned 'an eunuch or the virgin voice' and speaks as if winning over the crowds to his side were like 'schoolboy's tears', a 'beggar's tongue', 'inherent baseness' [III.ii.111–22]. The sexual analogies continue when a Roman speaking to a

Volscian about the banishment of Coriolanus says: 'the fittest
time to corrupt a man's wife is when she's fallen out with her
husband' [IV.iii.32–3].

Changing loyalties is sexual; Coriolanus speaks of his
allegiances in terms of love. Sexual feelings, affections and
social ties are intertwined. Thinking on the strange turn of
fate that has led him from fighting for Rome against the
Volsces to offering his services to the Volsces, he muses:

> Friends not fast sworn,
> Whose double bosoms seem to wear one heart,
> Whose hours, whose bed, whose meal and exercise
> Are still together, who twin, as 'twere, in love
> Unseparable, shall within this hour,
> On a dissension of a doit, break out
> To bitterest enmity. So fellest foes,
> Whose passions and whose plots have broke their
>     sleep
> To take the one the other . . .
> . . . shall grow dear friends
> And interjoin their issues. So with me:
> My birthplace hate I, and my love's upon
> This enemy town.
>
> [IV.iv.12–24]

## The sexuality of battle

When Coriolanus reveals himself to Aufidius the imagery is
erotic. The scene shows the bond between the two warriors
but the sexual content is unmistakable; the admiration of the
two warriors for each other is charged with homo-erotic
feelings:

> Let me twine
> Mine arms about that body, where against
> My grained ash a hundred times hath broke
> And scarred the moon with splinters. Here I clip
> The anvil of my sword, and do contest
> As hotly and as nobly with thy love

As ever in ambitious strength I did
Content against thy valour. Know thou first,
I loved the maid I married – never man
Sighed truer breath; but that I see thee here,
Thou noble thing, more dances my rapt heart
Than when I first my wedded mistress saw
Bestride my threshold.

[IV.v.110–22]

They have been dreaming of each other in images of violence which approach sexual fulfilment:

And I have nightly since
Dreamt of encounters 'twixt thyself and me –
We have been together in my sleep,
Unbuckling helms, fisting each other's throat –
And waked half dead and nothing.

[IV.v.126–30]

The line 'Your hand – most welcomed!' [IV.v.151], which many actors and directors have treated as the climax of the play, may be seen as Coriolanus' betrayal of Rome and himself; but it takes on a possible sexual significance as well. It is further foregrounded when the second servingman immediately says 'By my hand' [IV.v.153]. Thus we remember it when the third servingman soon says: 'Our general himself makes a mistress of him, sanctifies himself with's hand, and turns up the white o' th'eye to his discourse' [IV.v.203–5]. The notion of war as sexual energy can be seen in the remarks of the servingmen: 'Peace is . . . a getter of more bastard children . . . peace is a greater maker of cuckolds' [233–40]. War makes men bond together whereas peace makes men hate one another [241].

## The sexuality of domination

Aufidius' relationship to Coriolanus seems sexual not only in admiration but also in the desire to dominate. Whereas Coriolanus in his innocence and directness regards his relationship to Aufidius as that as a superior among equals, Aufidius is watchful, studying the Roman, waiting for a chance to reverse the defeats of the past. His language of dominance and conquest is sexual: 'When, Caius, Rome is thine, . . . then shortly art thou mine' [IV.vii.56]. If such sexuality is violent, predatory or part of admiration, love often implies influencing someone. When someone must persuade Coriolanus not to destroy Rome, it is someone who can use love to stop him. Affection has become a lever, a tool. Cominius is 'his general, who loved him' [v.i.2]. When the tribunes appeal to Menenius to plead with Coriolanus they say 'make trial what love can do' [v.i.40]. Why someone who loves Coriolanus would want to defend Rome is not clear. Menenius, however, has no hesitation to go on such an errand and brag to the Volsces that Coriolanus, 'is my lover' [v.ii.14]. Coriolanus admits 'I love thee' [v.ii.91], says that Menenius 'was my beloved in Rome' [v.ii.95] and speaks of the 'old love I have' for him [v.iii.12]. Whether or not such references have latent homosexual content, Coriolanus does not seem obsessed with sexual desire for women; he remains chaste in exile. His only tenderness towards Virgilia occurs in v.iii where we learn 'my true lip / Hath virgined it ever since' [47–8]. He is more concerned with his relationship to his mother than to his wife.

After Volumnia has conquered Coriolanus, Aufidius plays a similar role as conquerer. He has 'raised him' [v.vi.20] and claims Coriolanus has seduced his friends [v.vi.24], although Aufidius admits that he 'gave him away / In all his own desires' [33]. After Aufidius kills Coriolanus he 'stands on him' and is told 'tread not upon him' [v.vi.134], which while symbolic of dominance and a reversal of previous humiliation might – especially as we are told that Aufidius has drawn his sword – be seen as sexual.


## Power

Coriolanus shows power changing and the psychology of power – particularly how power reflects the needs of the people and society in different times and situations. Power is not stable, it shifts between the mob, Coriolanus, the tribunes, and Volumnia and finally, Aufidius. Power is sometimes gained by threats, by conquest, by demagoguery, by persuasion, by trickery – but inevitably power is created by men and women in specific situations and is not directly based on tradition, although ideas about institutions and traditions are part of the battle for power. Consider how power shifts. At first the dominance of the elite is challenged by the mobs who have been driven nearly to mutiny by the scarcity and cost of grain. This is an economic matter upon which the survival of the citizens depends. Faced by a possible revolt which would destroy their property and position, the nobility capitulate; they try to save what they can by compromise, offering cheap grain and the right of the commoners to have representation in the government. The compromise reveals weakness. Power cannot be shared unless there is a common interest, ideology, rhetoric, will, and so on. Protection of the state is such an interest in time of war; shared economic well-being is another.

Despite Menenius' claim that the state is an organic whole there is little reason to think many Romans in the play recognise shared class interests. At one extreme the tribunes only recognise the rights of the people (actually this means the tribunes' own status and power as elected representatives) while Coriolanus only recognises the rights of the nobles as the class which has built Rome in the past and which provides leadership in defence against enemy states. Power has shifted to the tribunes more than most of the nobles realise – although Coriolanus, who is blind in other ways, instinctively sees what has happened. The weakness of the nobles is soon proved when they are willing to sacrifice Coriolanus, their main hope of regaining power, rather than risk civil war. Before that, however, Coriolanus is momentarily brought close to power by single-handedly leading the troops to victory over the Volsces. His soldierly abilities are needed as long as there is an outside threat; short of taking arms and conquering Rome, he can govern only as part of a political process.

The tribunes, like Coriolanus, understand that there is an unfinished revolution in progress and that the nobles will not risk losing all their possessions in civil strife. Coriolanus sees what is happening and is unwilling to accede quietly to the change. Thus, Coriolanus' attempt to be approved to consularship brings to a crisis the implicit war between nobles and other classes. The tribunes know that they must by any means keep Coriolanus from the consularship as he is likely to lead a reaction. The conflict between the two major groups of the Romans is represented by the conflict between Coriolanus and the tribunes. Political conflicts and tests of strength are not abstract but are between individuals who in the historical process represent opposing groups. The tribunes know that the defence of their own power requires them to destroy Coriolanus; his unwillingness to compromise, his clear understanding of how power shifted with the creation of the tribunes, his popularity, strength of character and ability to unite men as soldiers make him dangerous, someone who by instinct and ability will defend what he considers a threatened older order. Coriolanus will fight for what he considers right. But his rigidity, his excess of virtue and his inability to use language hypocritically causes his downfall as it allows others to manipulate him into public displays of anger that alienate the populace.

The tribunes save and extend their power by persuading the citizens that their own liberties and rights are threatened. Faced by possible revolt, the nobles agree to deny Coriolanus the consularship; they agree to his trial and exile. The tribunes can convince others that Coriolanus is a threat because they and others think Coriolanus is no longer needed to defend the state; they want to believe that the Volsces, having been defeated, will not fight again. In their blindness to outside threats, they reveal a parallel one-sidedness to that of Coriolanus. He can understand only the world of war; they can imagine only a time of security. He despises those who will not fight; they imagine people naturally forming a community, protecting each other collectively through political rights, and they hate assertions of superiority. Although the action of the play would appear to support Coriolanus' view of the world, it also bears out that of the citizens. Or it could be said that both are wrong.

Power in the play shifts to the tribunes who have tested the nobility and found them without the will to resist. We learn, however, at IV.iii.20–7 that the banishment of Coriolanus has pushed some nobles to their limit and there is a possibility that if the tribunes go much further, the nobles might fight to restore the old order. The tribunes now appear conciliatory. When we next see them [IV.vi] they are being treated by the populace as their gods; the citizens kneel to them (the visual symbol of obedience) and pray for them. Their power, command of the political order and backing by the populace is only possible as long as it is not challenged by force since they and the citizens are not good soldiers. When Rome learns that Coriolanus is leading a foreign army, the tribunes immediately lose their power which shifts wildly among those nobles who are perceived as capable of persuading Coriolanus not to revenge himself.

In *Coriolanus* as in *Antony and Cleopatra* and in *Hamlet*, there is always an enemy army waiting to pounce on weakness; life is brutal, conquer or be conquered. These are not pacifist plays. Richard II's kingship is not able to resist Bolingbroke's greater will and force; legitimacy needs something more than right and justice if it is to govern. It requires the power to enforce its will and order. The nobles lacked such will before, now the tribunes lack power. When Coriolanus is persuaded by his mother not to attack Rome, power shifts to her and, ironically in the light of Coriolanus' failures, there is talk of making her consul. A parallel shift in power occurs among the Volsces. Aufidius, beaten in battle by Coriolanus and pushed aside from his leadership of the army, finds that after the compromise with Rome, he can now claim that Coriolanus is a traitor and then kill him with the aid of conspirators.

Shifts in power and tensions between legal authority and the actual force which governs is a central theme of the history plays; in *Coriolanus* the situation is more complex as popularity, legitimacy, loyalty, and power keep changing from moment to moment. In the tragedies, especially the Roman plays, people are mostly governed by self-interest; those who are not are usually the victims of others.

## Act V.vi

The conclusion of *Coriolanus* is curiously flat. Coriolanus, the only innocent among the leading characters, is savagely murdered and life goes on in its tasteless, base way. Aufidius, betrayer and murderer, rapidly says he is sorry (which we may doubt and think is another act of policy), reminds everyone that Coriolanus 'in this city. . . . Hath widowed and unchilded many a one' [151–2], 'Yet he shall have a noble memory', which grudging praise is depressing after we have watched Coriolanus for five acts. Even a villain deserves more sympathy. We know that historically the Volsces did indeed celebrate Coriolanus as a hero and honoured him after his death. Shakespeare purposefully played down those facts which might have given the play an up-beat ending and celebrated Coriolanus; he has denied the audience the feeling of satisfaction we expect at the end of tragedy. The ending of *Coriolanus* takes further the deflation and scepticism which Shakespeare has been practising in his tragedies. After Cleopatra's apparently triumphant death ('she looks like asleep / As she would catch another Antony / In her strong toil of grace'), the concluding speech by Caesar suddenly deflates what we have seen: 'her physician tells me / She hath pursued conclusions infinite / of easy ways to die'. After we have seen him plotting against Coriolanus, and indeed been warned earlier that he will use any means possible to 'potch at him' [I.x.15], it is hard to believe that Aufidius' 'rage is gone', or he is 'struck with sorrow'. But this takes us back to the whole dangerous problem of developing subtexts and character study, a method which Shakespeare's technique, with its excess of material supplied and lack of linkage between bits of information, invites. In the case of Aufidius we have enough information that a further novelisation of motives and psychology is likely to be in the realm of probability. From Act I.x onward we have been warned he wants to conquer Coriolanus by any means and we may assume that his behaviour from Act IV.v onwards is partly governed by craft. That would not prevent such emotions as the desire to beat Rome, admiration and homo-erotic feelings for Coriolanus, bitterness and resentment that Coriolanus has become the hero of the troops, outshines him as a leader of the Volsces soldiers, and treats him with less respect than he feels he deserves. In fact we are given information that Aufidius is awaiting his chance for revenge (a revenge that mirrors

Coriolanus' revenge against Rome). At the end of Act iv.vii there are two speeches in which Aufidius darkly says about Coriolanus that he has found means to 'break his neck' [iv.vii.25]. In the concluding speech of the scene Aufidius makes an analysis of Coriolanus' conduct in Rome and announces that when Coriolanus succeeds in defeating Rome he will soon be destroyed, 'then shortly art thou mine' [57].

We are not surprised when Aufidius turns from Coriolanus' rival into an Iago-like villain, directing a play in which Coriolanus finds himself, as in Rome, acting a dangerous part prepared for him. The ending might lead us to agree with Vickers' view that Coriolanus will 'destroy our complacency about politics forever'.

## Coriolanus' death

Is there any reason to assume that Coriolanus has no subtext, that he remains innocent about the ways of life, that he goes to his death like a charging bull that has not learned the cause of the moving cape? In Act v.iii when he gives in to his mother, he says that while she has won a victory for Rome:

> But for your son – believe it, O believe it –
> Most dangerously you have with him prevailed,
> If not most mortal to him. But let it come.
>                                            [187–9]

The way he appeals to Aufidius for approval indicates feelings that he has done wrong. 'Let it be' is Hamlet's phrase for accepting his fate. Why does Coriolanus return to face the Volsces in Corioli rather than go safely to Rome? He knows that trouble is expected and now behaves exactly as he should have in Rome when standing for the consularship. He knows how to use words and display to plead favour. He returns to the sound of drums and trumpets, and makes a speech which [v.vi.71–84] interprets his conduct in a more favourable light than is perhaps accurate. He made a 30 per cent profit in the campaign and shamed the Romans and has gone as far as the gates of Rome. This sounds good unless like the spectator and

Aufidius you know the truth. Coriolanus would not be doing this unless he too has learned cunning, policy and hypocrisy. You may feel he has now become human, that for the first time in the play you like him. Or you may feel this Coriolanus is just another politician, a former hero who soils the mad idealism of his past. Shakespeare's technique is such that he leaves the question open. After Aufidius calls him a 'boy of tears' Coriolanus reverts, as expected, to his enraged, insulting behaviour as he did twice in Rome. And as in Rome the people start to demand his death. History repeats itself.

Or does it? There is a strong possibility that Coriolanus expected this to happen and actually welcomes a chance to die. 'Cut me to pieces. . . . Stain all your edges on me.' He sees himself as a figure in history: 'If you have writ your annals true, 'tis there . . . I fluttered your Volscians in Corioles' [111–15]. 'Alone I did it.' Suicide? Someone like Othello trying to provide a last minute self-justification before death? The speech may at first look like the heroic stoic self-sufficiency of Act iii.iii ('I banish you'); but it can equally be read as a bit of play-acting by someone determined to control his own death, someone working on those whom he knows plan to kill him. I do not say this must be so. This is a possible reading, a reading either created by Shakespeare's technique – which allows multiple interpretations – or a reading sensitive to implications of the text, implications which suggest a new, emotional development in Coriolanus since his exile. There is Aufidius' odd claim that Coriolanus 'with dews of flattery seduced his friends' [v.vi.23]. Critics find this so unlikely of Coriolanus that they assume Aufidius is making excuses. But it could be true. At the play's end we still know little about Coriolanus' inner life or his life in exile. We really do not need, like modern Theorists, to deconstruct the text to be free from 'dead' readings. A Shakespearean play is so open in its possibilities that critics who claim a need for the freedom to deconstruct must be driven by other motives than the supposed prison of the text.

In many of Shakespeare's plays, especially in the tragic period, there is towards the end a suffering Christ-like figure. This may be a sacrificial woman, such as Desdemona or Cordelia, or a character who recalls Christ perhaps, like

Richard II, by some analogy formed in their own mind. The play may seem to reach towards an allegory or perhaps only recall a providential view, as in *Hamlet*, which some character comes to accept. In the Roman plays such a dimension is missing, as it should no doubt be. Yet if examined closely *Coriolanus* shows a few surprising traits at the conclusion in common with *Measure for Measure*, *King Lear*, and other plays with Christian themes. I am thinking of the importance of mercy and the way Coriolanus accepts his fate, 'let it come'. There is the possibility, as Kenneth Burke and others have suggested, that we regard Coriolanus as a sacrificial figure. This is in contrast with the cool pagan god-like revengeful Coriolanus, who is uncaring, unmerciful and bent on destruction. The gods in the play seem distant, cold, without mercy. They look down and laugh. We might say that Christianity is in the play as an erasure, a presence that has been removed but which is still felt by not being there:

MENENIUS.  He wants nothing of a god but eternity, and a heaven to throne in.
SICINIUS.  Yes, mercy, if you report him truly.

[v.iv.24–7]

## Comedy?

Ibsen referred to his *An Enemy of the People* as a comedy and G. B. Shaw, perhaps influenced by Ibsen, called *Coriolanus* a comedy. The play is not a comedy in the conventional sense of having an amusing, happy ending – unless you are a Roman – but there is an insight here that needs to be considered. Except for Coriolanus, this is not a play in which significant characters die. After an immense expenditure of energy in plots, attempted revenge, plans, nothing much changes. It is a play of repetition and anticlimax and people have been shown to be proud and vain; it is a demonstration of the vanity of human wishes and politicians and heroes.

The people, whether Roman or Volscian, one moment want to kill, the next worship, then soon again want to kill Coriolanus. Coriolanus enters Rome a conquering hero and is soon sent into perpetual exile; he enters Corioli a hero and is soon killed; the man no one can defeat in battles keeps giving in to his mother and even cries when she threatens to disown him. Volumnia raises her boy to be a hero, but she is finally the hero. The tribunes want Coriolanus banished so they can rule, but no sooner has he turned against Rome than they cannot defend the city and call him their countryman (instead of the enemy of the people). Menenius is so confident of his ability to win Coriolanus from destroying Rome that when he fails, he is unwilling to accept that Volumnia may have succeeded. But then the tribunes are unwilling to accept that Rome may be in danger; they are so proud of themselves that they want to whip the messenger rather than listen to the truth. Everyone of any importance in the play, except Coriolanus, is busy manipulating others, with usually what turns out to be disastrous effects. Nothing succeeds. Coriolanus does not become consul. Coriolanus does not destroy Rome. The tribunes find that political power is not finally true power. The one man whom Coriolanus admires turns out to be the most base of the lot. Farce? Cynicism? Disillusionment? Realism? It is a matter of tone. The tone is cool, distanced, epic, but the elements are indeed there for Ibsen's comedy.

## The politics of neo-classicism

*Coriolanus* was written during the early years of the formation of English neo-classicism, when Ben Jonson and others explored what use could be made of the classics for improving literary style, understanding human nature and political wisdom. The neo-classicism of the Stuart period was not merely cultural – architecture, literature and portraiture in painting – but also political. This is obvious later in the century when Roman analogies are invoked as often as biblical parallels to argue political positions by both Royalists and Republicans. The stereotypes of the later seventeenth century were being formed in the early Stuart period. Behind such a mode of imagination was the start of modern British history studies in the form of the antiquarianism of William Camden, the great scholar who was Ben Jonson's teacher. Camden attempted to collect information about English history with an awareness of its Roman period. (Camden's 1605 *Remains of a Greater Worke Concerning Britaine* is the basis of a few points in Menenius' fable of the belly.) The effect of this was to make modern Britain appear continuous with Rome; England now had a classical past, rather than the crazy quilt of late medieval English monarchy, an historically recognised past, a legitimacy (remember the tribunes anticipate that Coriolanus will claim his ancestors built Rome), and was part of Europe (a Stuart policy in contrast with Tudor isolationism). England was viewed as a continuation of Roman politics and rituals.

If Rome provided a model for the state, its laws (James was obsessed with Roman law) and the duties of the citizen, it also provided an historical model – examples of the dangers of republicanism, the fall into anarchy and tyranny. Such conservative ideas were in formation, being used, explored, but perhaps had not reached the clarity and fixedness they would achieve by the second half of the century. This does not mean that *Coriolanus* must be interpreted in a specific way. The play has a political context, but the context does not impose a specific argument on the text. A work of art reflects, mirrors is Shakespeare's word, social and political tensions, it seldom votes for a party.

Neo-classical influences can be seen in many of Shakespeare's plays, such as in *Othello* and *The Tempest* which concentrate the action in place and time, a concentration which contrasts to Shakespeare's manner in his history plays and *Antony and Cleopatra* or the highly formalised artifice of romance, as in *The Winter's Tale*. Superficially *Coriolanus* lacks classical unity; the location changes and covers an expanse of time. But the play feels classical and that has to do with something besides the setting. The focus on the main character and his obsession with virtue which destroys him is an adaptation of the Aristotelian notion of tragedy being about some good characteristic taken to an extreme which becomes a cause of tragedy. Coriolanus embodies too well values of his society: masculinity, valour, warfare, bravery. His tragedy is his truth to such virtue, his lack of moderation. In this play there is no secondary plot, rather there are plots by secondary characters which advance the main action and cannot be kept distinct from what Coriolanus does as he is often involved with or reacting against them. The restricted canvas space feels classical as it approximates the aim of classical unities.

Besides the focus on the hero there is the matter of tone, the play's distancing of its characters from our sympathy. Such distancing is inherent to epic technique and was learned from Shakespeare by Ibsen and Brecht; but there is a difference between such effects as inherent to a form and the conscious exploitation of distancing. Here distance and irony may at first appear objective until you realise that Shakespeare undermines (through what they say and what others say about them) every significant character in the play. What looks like objectivity is actually satiric. Satire was the main mode the Elizabethans learned from Rome.

The two plays *Coriolanus* most resembles are Ben Jonson's *Catiline* and *Sejanus*. They have a similar concentration on Roman politics, a flat, objective tone, a possible satiric intent. Shakespeare is not Jonson and there is evidence that his play was written and performed first; but we should see *Coriolanus* in the context both of Shakespeare's plays on classical, especially Roman history, and Jonson's satirical histories of Rome. There is a distinct Jacobean literary kind to which Coriolanus belongs and which is part of the English revival of interest in Roman culture and history.

## Social context

It is tempting to find analogies between the events of Coriolanus and late sixteenth–early seventeenth-century English history. The play concerns city mobs, the urban mobs that threatened Parliament throughout the seventeenth century, and which were led by dissenting members of Parliament. The characters on stage are mechanics, apprentices, shopkeepers, traders, not farm workers. The enclosure riots were the result of larger changes within the structure of English society and economics; they were part of the rationalisation of farming, which was in itself part of a movement towards greater centralisation in tax collecting, government, and so on. The kind of urban mutiny shown in the play belongs to the early modern world. The tribunes who represent the people have become a class in themselves. The situation in the play where no one class dominates, but in which there is unresolved potential civil war, is like early seventeenth-century England in which feudal power had been destroyed and the question remaining is whether the court or Parliament will rule.

*Coriolanus* mirrors the conflict between Parliament and court by showing a shift of power, a new class of people's representatives which threatens authority, a situation that is still unclear, and that the threat of mutiny has scared those in power. A state without clear leadership is in a bad condition and eventually the issue of dominance must be resolved one way or another. Coriolanus recognises there is a revolutionary situation and the granting of the tribunes is different from the ancient rights of the past to which the tribunes appeal. Coriolanus does not understand that his own appeal to tradition might be as revolutionary and modern as that of the tribunes.

But who are the rabble and their tribunes? Not who do they allegorise, but what social forces are mediated through them? While it is wrong to apply a modern class system to early seventeenth-century England, these citizens are probably the new petit bourgeoisie, the shopkeepers, tradesmen, craftsmen, of rapidly growing London. Then who are the tribunes? There is little evidence in the text but as they are familiar with law, history, the lives of the nobles, they are likely to be the new class of Inns of Court lawyers, who emerged in the century and who would lead the parliamentary forces in questioning the power of the king and the nobles. Such people were usually from landed families, younger sons, small farmers, freemen, those who had been excluded from nobility but who were better educated and of a higher social class than the mechanics and small shopkeepers. Such lawyers formed a definite block in Parliament.

This leaves such questions as what kind of political and social tensions found expression in Coriolanus? Why is he so aggressive about his rights as a noble? Why are they so specifically tied up with being a warrior? What social tensions are being mirrored or mediated? There are two distinctive themes here. Coriolanus feels he is part of a family that created

Rome, part of a group deriving from the founding fathers. Very few British nobles in the Jacobean period could in truth claim such a history as old nobility. The Tudors had a policy of eliminating the feudal lords through not naming new lords. Everything possible was done to diminish the number of lords so that by the time James I was crowned there were few titled nobles in England. Given early deaths, poor survival rates from illness, financial bankruptcy, it was sufficient merely not to appoint new lords to bring a class near extinction. Regarded in this way Coriolanus if he were British would have belonged to an endangered species around 1603. Coriolanus is concerned with his honour, his class, his freedom from contamination by those who lack his blood. If Coriolanus lived in a settled society where worth and title were recognised, he would not need to assert his class privileges and try to convince other nobles to fight to preserve their rights. Under Shakespeare's portrait of Rome are the social tensions of seventeenth-century England. Many of the Jacobean nobility had purchased or simply taken on themselves the titles of families that had died off or been ruined. A false pedigree purchased from those in charge of recording titles and a good marriage was enough to make a rich merchant into a noble within a generation. No wonder the nobles in *Coriolanus* are more familiar with the use of words than swords and when threatened by mob violence will compromise or sacrifice Coriolanus, the only real warrior among them.

The insecurity of the new class of nobles is reflected in the themes of the play, in the particians' claim to have a function whether as Menenius' belly or in the case of Coriolanus as warrior. The insecurity of the nobles is even more obviously reflected in the unsettled political situation of the play with its revolution in progress which challenges the nobles' right to power and the curious refusal of the nobility except Coriolanus to do more than temporise. There is no evidence from the play that this is a ruling class. The tribunes seem to have their own way throughout as do the Volsces except when Coriolanus fights for Rome. There is a gap. Where there should be a class and its instruments and its means of power, there is Coriolanus versus the mob and Coriolanus versus the outside enemy.

What begins as a play about food riots involves, I have suggested, a struggle between the urban mob plus the petit bourgeoisie led by a class of lawyers united against one man who represents the values of the nobility. The kind of political issue raised by the play would seem to refer to the relations between the king and Parliament. Both Coriolanus and the tribunes speak about the ancient rights of their class but in the situation as depicted in the play there are no real ancient rights at stake; there is a new conflict between the tribunes' desire to rule in the name of the people and Coriolanus' wish to destroy the power of the tribunes before they can extend their power to governing. This becomes clear after Coriolanus is exiled. The citizens pay the tribunes the respect and homage given to governors. The tribunes know from the first that if Coriolanus is given a consularship they are doomed and a counter-revolution will take place destroying their new power. Either he governs or they govern. The situation is clear when Coriolanus leads the Volscian army against Rome. No one can stop him. More important, he, unlike the historical Coriolanus, makes no distinction between the plebs and the nobility in his revenge.

## Coriolanus and monarchy

There is an important issue involved in Coriolanus' claim that government cannot be mixed and that someone must rule. English monarchy had traditionally been understood on the model of the king's two bodies. The king is more than a person. The king or queen rules in and only with the approval of Parliament. The Stuarts, however, had a continental notion of kingship and claimed a divine right to rule. Indeed they often ruled without Parliament, which they avoided calling. Kingship was looked upon by the Stuarts as an inheritance.

Coriolanus embodies the new Stuart notion of patriarchical rights of the king. The ancient rights he claims were in Stuart times new claims to supreme power; just as the ancient rights of the people as expressed by the tribunes turn out to be a new power. The tribunes claim a right to veto and a right to arrest anyone who defies them, as representatives of the people. In practice this is the right to govern, or at least to stop others governing. Coriolanus is like an early Stuart king denying the rights of Parliament to any say in government. Why are the other nobles in the play so unwilling to risk war? Because for them the distinction between ruler and ruled is less clear. They are more political than Coriolanus, but in their mind the question of who rules is not an either/or situation. They have no plans to reverse the new situation – beyond putting Coriolanus on the consul – because for them the government is either mixed or as true conservatives they can live with changes. Coriolanus cannot. For him government is inherited and is a right to be supreme.

The play as a mirror of the time has at its core the supreme issue of seventeenth-century politics, who will rule. The nobility do not count except as supporters of Coriolanus. Either the people's representatives will rule or this one man will rule in the name of inherited right. *Coriolanus* is a mirror of the times, an embodiment of political tensions which will be played out clearly within forty years.

## Conclusion

I began with problems raised by the distancing effect of *Coriolanus* which prevents sympathy or empathy with any character or group. While each person in the play has qualities possible to like, or at least agree with, they have stronger characteristics or views which audiences will hate. Moreover our perspective keeps changing or the character changes; but the changes take place outside our vision so that we only see the results, not the reasons for them. Such distancing is inherent to the epic sweep that the Elizabethan theatre inherited from the Mysteries; but it is also clear that during the late tragic period Shakespeare was experimenting with theatrical form, pointing to effects he wants, using verbal pictures, shifting the perspective through the eyes of a character (such as Cordelia in the division of the kingdom scene in *King Lear*). There is also the classicism; this is a play without subplot, without clowns and without addresses to the audience.

One effect of such distancing and classicism is to reduce

the spiritual ring around the play; it has no cosmology, offers no sense of the purpose of life. It is a play in which life is secular, materialist, a struggle for power and goods. Essential values, the individual, honour, virtue, pride, selfhood, are called into doubt and shown not only to be useless in the predatory world in which people gang up to get what they as a group desire, but the victors gain little. If Shakespeare in *Coriolanus* could be said to offer proof of the logic of cultural materialism, he could also be said to show why such a view is demoralising. This has led some critics to speculate whether we should not turn the play inside out and say that because the pagan world is awful *Coriolanus* indirectly preaches Christianity. It could, however, be argued that the scepticism and futility carries further a vision found in the tragedies of this period, that it is no different from, say, *King Lear*, as a statement about the terrors of reality.

A secular modern view is seen in the political focus, the class struggle, the way the play shows Rome divided and constantly threatened by others. In such a world, Coriolanus' pride is almost surreal, he is a Martian from another planet or era, an old-fashioned warrior hero in an age and culture of materialism. Yet this materialism is called into doubt as a final end of existence by the way the characters and mobs are driven by the need for love. The crowds want to be loved, and when not loved become murderers, just as Coriolanus has been made a warrior by his cold mother. This relationship of love to hate, of care and aggression seems at least an equal fact of life as the material world. If it is tempting to construct fictions about the relationship of *Coriolanus* to Jacobean politics and culture, the text is capable of a complexity of interpretation and yet is grounded in the most basic, most universal of emotions, our desires for love, our feelings of dependency, our anger and rage when care is denied, our need to be fed both food and affection. The moral tale we might want to construct remains open, but this most distant and cold of plays recounts the story of a society and a great man driven by lack of love.

Art depends on the renewal and progress of conventions. In *Coriolanus* Shakespeare has updated what Waith (1962) calls the Herculean Hero – Tamburlaine, the untamed, all-conquering warrior – put him in a society and examined such unbridled individualism and primitive virtue in political society. In the process the warrior has become a victim of psychology as well as, by a reversal of historical roles, representative of both modern individualism and the absolutism of James I. Interpretations can and will pile up relentlessly as we move, or history moves, Shakespeare's play through other contexts and further new cultural perspectives. Its greatness is its inner richness of imagery, political debate, irony, suggested characterisation, theatricality – a richness which is bound to result in multiple perspectives since the text will offer evidence to support many readings and methodologies. The mirroring, parallels, cross-cutting, changing focus and distance are characteristic of much late Renaissance, early Baroque art and especially of Jacobean drama; but we readily find such characteristics in *Coriolanus* because modernist and post-modernist styles have taught us to seek open, unstable texts. It is agreed that the Roman plays lack a religious dimension, but Cavell's (1985) brilliant essay worries the text to discover a radical inversion of the rituals of communion, a tell-tale erasure so strong that it will be difficult to ignore in future criticism of the play, especially as it can be linked to earlier insights by Siegel, Simmons and Burke. Having pressed the text so hard there is no way we can stop, no return to innocence. That is the glory, frustration and absurdity of criticism, especially of interpretative criticism. Formalist criticism is also influenced by the approach brought to the text, but as can be seen from the criticism of Wilson Knight, is more likely to be objectively descriptive. Objectively descriptive. An impossibility as words can never imitate what they describe.

There is no one correct interpretation of *Coriolanus* or any text. We cannot know the author's intent, what his age understood by the play, or even expect most other readers or stage-goers in our time to agree as to its significance. Such a bleak view assumes that the language of the text is there, but it has no fixed relationship to some original significance. What relationship it might have had is made more unstable by historical changes and the various conflicting elements (word play, politics, psychology, relationships to other texts, etc.) within the text. We can even question is there a text? What exactly did Shakespeare write? Who wrote the stage directions?

How accurate and accurate of what is the first printing?

If radical scepticism destroys the text, leaving nothing but scepticism, literary life goes on and most interpretations of *Coriolanus* seem to refer to the same play and use the same or similar evidence, even though the data are differently interpreted. Unless we are committed to radical scepticism, a text is there, but the questions we ask of it change what we read. Our answers are inscribed in our questions. If words can never precisely describe *Coriolanus* – just as we cannot precisely describe a landscape or an emotional experience – there is no description without the attempt. Each critic has a responsibility to work towards clear accurate descriptions of the play and its elements while being aware that any copy or analysis of reality is bound to be limited. If interpretation is a form of fiction-making at least we can try to be accurate and humble. If our maps of reality are bound to be wrong they benefit by being made with an awareness that the critical methods we employ are themselves sources of distortion while being necessary. That's life in the post-modern age.

# References

*Contextual approaches*

Leigh Holt, 'From Man to Dragon: A Study of Shakespeare's *Coriolanus*', *Salzburg Studies in English Literature*, LXI (1976).

E. C. Pettet, '*Coriolanus* and the Midland Insurrection of 1607', *Shakespeare Survey*, III (1950) 34–42.

Geoffrey Bullough (ed.), *Narrative and Dramatic Sources of Shakespeare: The Roman Plays. Vol. V* (London, 1966).

T. J. B. Spencer, 'Shakespeare and the Elizabethan Romans', *Shakespeare Survey*, X (1957), 27–38.

Edwin Honig, '*Sejanus* and *Coriolanus*: A Study in Alienation', *Modern Language Quarterly*, XII (1951), 407–21.

Clifford C. Huffman, '*Coriolanus' in Context* (Lewisburg, Pa., 1971).

Paul N. Siegel, *Shakespeare in His Time and Ours* (London, 1968).

*Formal approaches: character and imagery*

A. C. Bradley, 'Coriolanus' (1912) in *A Miscellany* (London, 1929).

Brian Vickers, *Shakespeare: Coriolanus* (London, 1976).

John Bayley, 'The Thing I Am: *Coriolanus*' in *Shakespeare and Tragedy* (London, 1981) pp. 147–63.

John Palmer, *The Political Characters of Shakespeare* (London, 1945) also in: John Palmer, *Political and Comic Characters of Shakespeare* (London, 1965).

G. Wilson Knight, 'The Royal Occupation. An Essay on *Coriolanus*' in *The Imperial Theme* (Oxford, 1931; 3rd edn, London, 1951).

Caroline Spurgeon, *Shakespeare's Imagery and What It Tells Us* (New York, 1935).

L. C. Knights, *Some Shakespearian Themes* (Stanford, 1960).

Derek A. Traversi, *An Approach to Shakespeare* (1938 2nd edn 1956; Garden City, 3rd edn 1969).
Maurice Charney, *Shakespeare's Roman Plays: The Function of Imagery in Drama* (Cambridge, Ma., 1961) pp. 142–97.

*Religious, sociological and anthropological approaches*
J. L. Simmons, *Shakespeare's Pagan World: The Roman Tragedies* (Charlottesville, Va., 1973; Brighton, 1974).
Kenneth Burke, *Language as Symbolic Action* (Los Angeles, 1966).
Jan Kott, 'Coriolanus or Shakespearean Contradictions' in *Shakespeare Our Contemporary* (Garden City NY, 1964) pp. 133–62.
Gail Kern Paster, 'To Starve with Feeding: Shakespeare's Idea of Rome' in *The Idea of the City in the Age of Shakespeare* (Athens, Ga., 1985) pp. 58–90.

*Interdisciplinary approaches: Marxist and psychoanalytical*
Terry Eagleton, *William Shakespeare* (Oxford, 1986).
Jonathan Dollimore, *Radical Tragedy: Religion, Ideology and Power in the Drama of Shakespeare and his Contemporaries* (Chicago, 1984).
Charles K. Hofling, 'An Interpretation of Shakespeare's *Coriolanus*', *American Imago*, 14 (Spring 1957) 411–31.
Janet Adelman, 'Anger is My Meat: Feeding, Dependency, and Aggression in *Coriolanus*' in *Representing Shakespeare* eds Murray M. Schartz and Coppelia Kahn (Baltimore, 1980) pp. 129–49.

*Theatre approaches: performances and transpositions*
Ralph Berry, 'The Metamorphoses of *Coriolanus*' in *Changing Styles in Shakespeare* (London, 1981).
John Dryden, *All for Love* (1678).
Henrik Ibsen, *An Enemy of the People* (Preface by Martin Esslin) English adaptation by Max Faber (London, 1967).
T. S. Eliot, 'Coriolan' (1931).
Arthur Miller's adaptation of *An Enemy of the People* by Henrik Ibsen (New York, 1951).
Bertold Brecht, 'Study of the First Scene of Shakespeare's

*Coriolanus'* in *Brecht on Theatre* ed. John Willet (London, 1964).

*Appraisals*

Bernard Beckerman, *Shakespeare at the Globe: 1599–1606* (New York, 1962).

J. L. Styan, *Shakespeare's Stagecraft* (Cambridge, 1967).

Eugene M. Waith, 'Coriolanus' in *The Herculean Hero* (New York, 1962) pp. 121–43.

Stanley Cavell, 'Who Does the Wolf Love? Coriolanus and the Interpretations in Politics' in *Shakespeare and the Questions of Theory*, eds Patricia Parker and Geoffrey Hartman (New York, 1985) pp. 245–72.

# Selected Bibliography

B. A. Brockman (ed.), *Coriolanus: A Casebook* (London, 1977, reprint 1982, 1983).

Reuben A. Brower, 'The Deeds of Coriolanus', *Hero and Saint* (New York, 1971) pp. 354–81.

David Daniell, *Coriolanus in Europe* (London, 1980).

Alan Dessen, 'Shakespeare and Theatrical Conventions' in *The Cambridge Companion to Shakespeare Studies* (Cambridge, 1986).

Bruce King, *Macmillan History of Seventeenth-Century English Literature* (London, 1982).

James E. Phillips (ed.), *Twentieth Century Interpretations of Coriolanus* (Englewood Cliffs, NJ, 1970).

Stanley Wells (ed.), *The Cambridge Companion to Shakespeare Studies* (Cambridge, 1986).

# Index

Page numbers in italics indicate the main discussion of a critic or theme.

Adelman, Janet  *48–50*, 109
*All for Love*  54
*Antony and Cleopatra*  14, 25, 26, 65, 73, 93, 94, 99
Aristotle  99
Aufidius  18, 26, 42, 47, 48, 51, 52, 57, 65, 66, 70, 74–5, 76, 81, 82, 83, 84, 85, 86, 88, 89, 90, 91, 93, 94, 96
Austen, Jane  17

Bayley, John  *21–2*, 24, 108
Beckerman, Bernard  *60–1*, 67, 110
Benson, F. R.  51
Berry, Ralph  *50–2*, 109
Blackfriars theatre  15
Borges, J. C.  11, 46
Bradley, A. C.  10, *17–21*, 23, 24, 28, 30, 108
Brecht, Bertold  10, 37, 53, 57, 58, 62, 66, 100, 109–10
Brockman, B. A.  111
Brower, Reuben  111
Bullough, Geoffrey  14, 108
Burke, Kenneth  28, *34–7*, 39, 40, 44, 66, 97, 106, 109

Calvin, John  33, 34
Camden, William  14, 98–9
*Catiline*  14, 100
Cavell, Stanley  106, 110
Charney, Maurice  31, 109
christian  15, 16, 24, *31–4*, 46, 65, 68, 73, 96–7, 105
citizens  11, 18, 39, 64, 74, 85, 86
Cominius  26, 62, 64, 65, 83, 84, 90

criticism, practical  11, 21
criticism, reception  11

Dennis, John  53
Dessen, Alan  111
Dollimore, Jonathan  16, *46–8*, 109
Dryden, John  53–4, 109

Eagleton, Terry  44, *45–6*, 109
Eliot, T. S.  11, 28, 53, 55–6, 109
enclosures  14, 100
*Enemy of the People*  55, 97, 109

Freud, S.  48

Globe theatre  15, *60–1*, 67
Guthrie, Tyrone  51

*Hamlet*  13, 18, 19, 31, 62, 73, 93, 97
Hercules  77–8, 105
Hofling, C. K.  48, 109
Holt, Leigh  14, 108
Honig, Edwin  14, 108
Huffman, Clifford  14, 15, 108
Humanism  16, 39, 46, 56

Ibsen, Henrick  53, *54–5*, 56, 57, 97, 100, 109

Jacobean  17, 60, 102, 105
Jacobean drama  16, 82, 106
James I  14, 15, 16, 17, 99, 102, 106
Johnson, Samuel  20
Jonson, Ben  14, 16, 98, 100

*Julius Caesar*  14, 38, 41
Juno  78

Kemble, John P.  50
King, Bruce  111
*King Lear*  13, 19, 35, 73, 74, 75, 77, 96, 97, 104, 105
King's Men  15
Knight, G. Wilson  *24–9*, 30, 83, 106, 108
Knights, L. C.  24, *29–30*, 61, 108
Kott, Jan  *37–41*, 44, 46, 109

Lacan  44
Lawrence, D. H.  17
Leavis, F. R.  24, 30
Livy  40–1

Marxist  13, 16, 33, *37–41*, *44–8*, 56, 58
*Measure for Measure*  19, 31, 73, 97
Menenius  14, 21, 22, 23, 25, 26, 30, 35, 42, 49, 61, 74, 76, 77, 79, 80, 82, 85, 91, 97, 98, 99, 102
Miller, Arthur  53, *56–7*, 109

Neville, John  51

Olivier, Laurence  51
Osborne, John  53, 56
*Othello*  19, 26, 65, 68, 74, 75, 77, 96, 99

Palmer, John  *22–3*, 108
Paster, Gail Kern  *41–3*, 66, 109
Pettet, E. C.  14, 15, 108
Phillips, James  111
Plutarch  14, 23, 32, 41, 53
Proust  17

Renaissance  46, 60
revenge  16, 48, 65
*Richard II*  18, 31, 93, 97
*Richard III*  75
Roman plays  14, 91, 93, 97, 100, 106, 108

*Scrutiny*  24, 30
*Sejanus*  14, 100, 108
Shaw, G. B.  97
Sicinius  38–9, 82, 97
Siegel, Paul  16, 106, 108
Simmons, J. L.  *31–4*, 106, 109
Smirnov, A. A.  44
Spencer, T. J. B.  14, 108
Spurgeon, Caroline  25, 108
Styan, J. L.  *61–4*, 110

*Tamburlaine*  39
Tate, Nahum  53
*The Tempest*  75, 99
*Timon of Athens*  36
Traversi, Derek  *30*, 108
tribunes  11, 47, 69, 76, 82

Valeria  28, 62, 63
Vickers, Brian  21, 95, 108
Virgilia  28, 31, 38, 78, 81, 82, 83, 90
Volumnia  20, 28, 40, 42, 46, 48, 49, 50, 54, 61, 63, 66, 69–70, 76, 77, 78, 79, 80, 81, 82, 83, 85, 87, 91, 98

Wells, Stanley  111
*Winter's Tale*  77, 99

Yeats, Y. B.  56